Pinky & I

THE FORMATIVE YEARS

Elizabeth "Robin" Perry

BALBOA.PRESS

A DIVISION OF HAY HOUSE

Balboa Press books may be ordered through booksellers or by contacting:

Balboa Press
A Division of Hay House
1663 Liberty Drive
Bloomington, IN 47403
www.balboapress.com
844-682-1282

Because of the dynamic nature of the Internet, any web addresses or
links contained in this book may have changed since publication and may
no longer be valid. The views expressed in this work are solely those
of the author and do not necessarily reflect the views of the publisher,
and the publisher hereby disclaims any responsibility for them.

The author of this book does not dispense medical advice or prescribe
the use of any technique as a form of treatment for physical, emotional,
or medical problems without the advice of a physician, either directly
or indirectly. The intent of the author is only to offer information
of a general nature to help you in your quest for emotional and
spiritual well-being. In the event you use any of the information in
this book for yourself, which is your constitutional right, the author
and the publisher assume no responsibility for your actions.

Any people depicted in stock imagery provided by Getty Images are
models, and such images are being used for illustrative purposes only.
Certain stock imagery © Getty Images.

Print information available on the last page.

ISBN: 978-1-9822-5490-2 (sc)
ISBN: 978-1-9822-5491-9 (e)

Balboa Press rev. date: 01/06/2021

Contents

Acknowledgements

First and foremost, I give thanks to you Creator, Cherisher and Sustainer of us all! Thank you for my being. Thank you for my parents. Thank you for my siblings, my children, and my progeny. Thank you for all that you have done for my life and in my life... Thank you!

I also want to Thank my dear sister friend "Ast Maat" aka Sandra McIntyre! Thank you for your endless encouragement and support. Thank you for the proofing and all that you did and endured to help me make it through this monumental effort. Thank you!

I want to thank my darling son Abdul-Maalik Perry for his proofing and editing advice. The questions and suggestions really took this book to a whole new level for me and I thank you so much for your selfless commitment to my success in finishing this project. Thank you!

I want to thank "Joanne Scott" for her support of this work and for her continued friendship over the years. You were and shall remain my "other" big sister. I wish you and yours nothing but God's Best! Thank you!

Finally, I want to give "Thanks" and hope to Pinky, her children, and countless grandchildren. May you appreciate and have a sense of Pinky! She is ever present and still looking out for us all. She will always be loved and never forgotten!

I want to give a very special thank you to Mr. Thomas Purwin. Your contribution is priceless; as is your friendship. "Thank you Sir!"

Brook, my gift from Pinky! Thank you for all of the love. You remind me so much of your mother and have allowed me to step in and be like a mother to you. I pray that Pinky and you find me ready and eager to be there for you like your mother was there for my life.

I know that your mother is very proud of you and your brothers and watches over all of you. Thank you!

Preface

I think it must happen to everyone at some point or another. You navigate life to a point where you finally figure out that everything is as it was meant to be and it all started... someplace. If you can pinpoint the time and place it started, or when you became aware of it starting, you may be able to find the answers to the mysteries of your journey.

If you think my start came with the advent of being born, it didn't. It also didn't come from the split-up of my parents, or the life lessons of cleaning and cooking that my mother taught me before she left. My awareness came when my older sister took me by the hand and we crossed the street! That's when I knew nothing and no one would be able to "stop" this life-long journey.

Although my sister was one year older than I, her bravery and wits were ageless. By standing up for me and allowing me to experience life under her, she gave me wings. My childhood adventures were better than my Tom Sawyer and Heidi books because my adventures with Pinky were not fiction. They shaped and moulded my future using her affirming and vibrant experiences as a sister and friend to others.

Pinky was not my first teacher (my mother was), but she sure was a close second. Surviving those first couple of years without our mother was very hard! Luckily our mother had left us with some family values and lessons to live by; and as anyone can tell you Pinky most definitely was my first hero!

Pinky took great care of us; we all took great care of each other. But there is something about being able to move through the world knowing that someone has your back and will do anything for you. It is even more amazing when the person that steps up for you is not supposed to be able too.

Pinky was supposed to have been limited in her abilities because of lead poisoning; but like in the case of any hero; wherever there is a compromised ability there is a super power to replace it. Pinky's super power was fearlessness! She was not afraid of anything, or at least she never showed it. She was loyal and committed to her family and friends and at the time of these memories she was only eight years old. Eight going on twenty!

She willed to me a sense of fearlessness and an understanding of commitment and loyalty. I love her and miss those days that did so much to inform and shape me. I'm thankful that through this book I was able to see why the memories have always remained so vivid. I hope others will go ahead and allow their memories to flow. That they will find that point where they entered into their being; and that they will allow the emotions shaped way back when to inform them for their now, today.

You have a sister (or brother), someone who held your hand, who did the most they could for you to be here now? You have/had someone that would have died for you? Or you for them? Whether they are alive or have transcended this life; think of them. Remember them. Tell others about them; and give thanks for them and to them!

I thank the Creator each and every day for the life and times of my Big Sister "Pinky," May she rest in peace!

Foreword by Ast Ma'at

Whether it's obvious to us or not, we often hold, within ourselves, undetected opinions and imagery around many aspects of life. Until something jars loose the view we have long held, our perspective remains static.

Pinky and I is a delightful tale of devotion, resilience and the unassuming pursuit of joyous life; in the face of some woefully challenging and sometimes heart wrenching circumstances, where most might never expect to find it.

Exactly where I was _not_ looking for innocence and insatiable zest for life is precisely where _Pinky and I_ delivered just that! Lured in, I found myself in an expansive journey through the eyes of a 7 year old little girl who was completely in awe of her amazing older, big sister, best friend, protector and guide.

What is unexpectedly poignant about this memoir is the circumstances and conditions; over which these two tiny people had no influence or control, that caused the amazing bond and unshakable love to expand and deepen for them.

Much goes awry in their lives and yet, even through the dichotomy of fundamental choices they make, the foundation of love and values their mother imparted guides them and makes witnessing their adventures and challenges

(-their journey-) quite thought provoking, entertaining and compassion inducing. _Pinky and I_ is much too short. I'd love to follow their story further!

Thank you. Sandra A. McIntyre / Ast Ma'at

Chapter 1

"No she ain't going and that's that," said Jenny.

"Oh yeah, says who?" asked Pinky.

"Says my two friends right here," Jenny said as she showed her two fists balled up tight.

"Well tap off then," said Pinky, her hands held out waiting for the slap that would signal the beginning of the fight. Jenny looked at Pinky, and then she looked at Robin, then back to Pinky again. "Aaah forget it, but she's your problem!"

"Alright," Pinky said, backing off. "Come on," she said, grabbing at Robin's hand and pulling her along. "Listen now; you know why they don't want you to come?" Robin shook her head, "yes!"

"Okay so you gotta not be scared!" Pinky said as she gave Robin a tug.

"I'm not scared," Robin said as she pulled her arm away from Pinky.

"Good, I tell you what! You can be the look-out, how about that?"

"Okay," Robin said shyly.

"Good! Now when we go into the store you just keep looking around like you looking for something."

"Like what?"

"I don't know; like you're looking for a card for ma's birthday! Yeah a card, okay?" asked Pinky.

"Okay!" said Robin, feeling a bit more sure of herself, her confidence building.

"Now if anyone comes near us you just wave your hand and we will leave! Then you just come outside and we'll get you; alright?" Pinky asked.

"Alright," said Robin. She didn't want to mess this up. Every time her big sister would let her hang something would go wrong and Pinky's friends would get mad at both of them. Then they wouldn't want Robin to come along. Pinky would always stand up for her, but sometimes even Pinky would get discouraged with her. Robin didn't care about hanging with "them" as much as she liked being with Pinky. Pinky was only a year older than Robin; but to Robin, Pinky was her hero! As far as Robin was concerned Pinky wasn't afraid of anything! She always did the coolest things and had the courage to make friends with everybody. But most importantly Pinky and Robin shared a secret bond... they were with their mother the day she had to leave.

They all went two and two into the Five & Dime store and met up at the hair supply aisle. Jenny and Barbara got busy filling their pockets with the hair bows and pins. Jenny even managed to stuff a ponytail into the back of her pants. Robin was trying to watch everything and her nerves were starting to get the best of her. Pinky had managed to get a fair share of hair bows and 'two' ponytails tucked away before everything started going awry. Pinky had been stashing her goods and keeping an eye on Robin at the same time. A store clerk had noticed Robin and was walking towards her! Robin had, by now, lost all her nerve. She mindlessly picked up a jar of Dixie Peach hair grease, too confused to wave.

"Look out!" Robin yelled as the lady came near. With that she dropped the hair grease. The signal wasn't what they planned but the girls got the point and started to cool, calm, and collectively go out of the store. The store clerk had thought that Robin was trying to warn 'her' and she jumped back to avoid the shattering glass and the spillage of its contents.

"Thank you," said the young store clerk lady. Robin had shock and fear all over her face. The store clerk consoled her "It's okay! I'm okay. Are you okay?" she asked, leaning in and giving Robin a quick look over.

"Yes, I'm okay" Robin said quietly. "I'm sorry; I didn't mean to break your hair grease." Robin said as she started walking, heading straight for the door.

"No worries, never you mind about that, it's not as if you were planning to take it without paying," the clerk was now saying rather loudly as Robin was on her way out the door. Robin stopped, turned and looked at the lady clerk questioningly for a quick second. She waved goodbye to the lady and the lady waved back. When she got outside, she walked away from the front of the store and started looking around. She spotted Jenny and Barbara across the street and Jenny was pointing for her to walk towards the corner. As she got near the corner Pinky came up from behind and gave her a big ole hug. "You did it girl! You're the best look out ever." And she gently shoved her aside. "What took you so long?"

"I don't know," Robin said shyly. "The lady was nice."

"Yeah, well... Guess what we got?!" she said as she started pulling out all kinds of ponytail holders and barrettes. Robin's eyes were bigger than usual as she looked over the loot she helped her big sister to steal.

The girls were altogether now and they had made it to the park. They decided to rest for a minute. All three girls were looking over their illustrious booty. After a minute of oohing and ah-ing Pinky said, "and to the coolest lookout ever, I present to you these fine jewels," as she gave Robin a pair of rhinestone studded Bobby Pins..."and"... she said as she looked over to Jenny and Barbara, nodding her head toward Robin as their cue to give her little sister something from their booty as well.

"What?!" said Jenny, "I told you she was your problem."

"Yeah!" said Barbara in agreement.

"Yeah, but she wasn't a problem. She was a lookout, and lookouts get looked out for; so divvy-up," Pinky said sternly.

Jenny and Barbara looked at each other, then they looked at Robin.

"Yeah, the little Pip-Squeak came through, you're right," said Jenny handing Robin a package of the big ball ponytail holders in jewel tone colors. Barbara agreed and gave her the same thing, but in black and white.

"Thank you!" Robin said, happy to be rewarded.

"You're welcome," the girls all said in unison.

Then Pinky took her to the side and said, "Hey listen, you take these for you and the girls, but don't let Marybelle know you got them. If she finds out, tell her that you bought them, okay?"

"Okay," Robin said.

"Uh...Oh, what's this?" Pinky said as she slowly pulled out the two ponytail wigs and waved them in front of Robin's face. Robin brushed at them because they were tickling her face. She laughed as she tried to grab them and Pinky kept snatching them away. "Here," and she tossed one to her! "Hold it for me. Will you?"

"Yeah, of course I will, but what about Marybelle?" Marybelle was their grandmother.

"Hide it with the hair bows, I'm counting on you," Pinky said.

"Okay! You can count on me," Robin said proudly. Pinky was Robin's number one hero. Pinky could fight. She knew how to do the coolest things and Pinky was always going places. About the only thing Pinky didn't like was staying at her grandmother's house. So at just eight years old Pinky was coming and going as she pleased, as she "needed" to...

Chapter 2

"Y'all hurry up and go on outside!" Marybelle was yelling from the other room. "Robin did you finish Dunk's hair?" she also yelled out.

"Yes!" Robin yelled back as she was just finishing up and pushing Dunk from between her legs. "Go on, and keep your hands out of your hair," she whispered to Dunk.

"I will," Dunk said as she ran away shaking her head from side to side. Robin was clearing away the supplies she used to slick down the girls' hair and make the beautiful, full ponytails. She put the hard brush and ponytail holders in the shoebox which she kept tucked under the bed. She put the Dixie Peach hair grease on the shelf above the chest of drawers. She was walking towards the kitchen with the glass of water that had been made cloudy from the greasy hair brush when her Aunt Nita stopped her. Nita was only six years older than Robin but because of her size and weight; she seemed to be an adult over her. She liked acting like one too.

"Where are you going?"

"I'm going to put this glass away; then outside."

"You feel like going to the store for me," Nita asked?

"Are you paying?" Robin asked.

"Yeah Greedy, how much do you want?"

"A dime; and you shouldn't be calling anybody greedy, with your fat self." Robin retorted.

When Robin first got to her grandmother's house she used to be afraid of Nita, because Nita used to always take advantage of Robin and her sisters. She used to take their snacks and make them do her chores. Pinky didn't like it so one day she fought Nita and got the better of her. Then Pinky told Nita if Robin or any of her sisters cried because of her she was going to whoop her butt. So Nita might say some things every now and then but she doesn't make them cry and Robin just tries to be as tough as her sister. But secretly, Robin prays that Nita doesn't hurt her.

Robin put away the jar and Nita was waiting with her list of things she wanted.

"Get me a bag of chips, a milk bar, 5 cents worth of candy coins and five cents worth of two for a penny cookies," she said as she handed Robin a quarter and five pennies.

"Where is my dime?"

"I'll pay you when you get back."

"No, I don't trust you." Robin said.

"What do you mean you don't trust me, you calling me a liar?"

"I'm not calling you a liar. I just don't trust you so you need to give me the dime now." Robin said.

"Here, take this money and go to the store. Ain't nobody gonna trick you. I said I will pay you when you get back. Now hurry up before I tell Momma you're in here calling people liars." Nita said as she gently pushed Robin out the door.

Downstairs Robin stopped on the wooden stoop with its concrete steps and concrete platform below. She was just about to jump from the top step down to the concrete platform when she heard Mrs. James speaking to her through her first floor screened in window.

"Hey there Robin. How you doing? You feel like doing some cleaning?"

"Yes ma'am!" Robin said, excited to make a couple of dollars, which is what Mrs. James always paid, no matter what she did. Mrs. James had four children and was married to a mortician. Many people called her and her children strange but Robin didn't care about that kind of stuff. She enjoyed making money; and playing with the children sometimes. Her children, two girls and two boys, were all younger than Robin and rumored to still wear diapers. The oldest boy, her first born, was called 'retarded'. He often talked out loud to himself and had a strange habit of licking his hands and streaking his face with his saliva. Robin didn't like that. But other than that they were just like her little sisters, fun to play with "sometimes". As she came into the house she had to wait for Mrs. James to put her two big German Shepherd dogs away. They always got riled up when anyone would come into the house. Mrs. James said that's what makes them good watch dogs. Robin just thought they were hungry and would love to eat her up. She was afraid of them.

"You can start with the dishes first," said Mrs. James.

"Okay."

She ran water into the dish pan and watched the children as they played with their food at the table. JJ was four years old and seeminged very smart. "You wanna color my green hornet book with me, it's new?"

"Maybe later." Robin said.

"Alright," he said getting up, leaving the table covered in watery red sauce. His two younger sisters followed equally covered in the red sauce. The oldest boy Charles did not leave the table, he just sat there mumbling something and wiping his eye with his spit covered hand repeatedly. As she had cleared the table she examined their bowls. The canned spaghetti with meatballs had an awful lot of water added to it! Robin found some meatballs left in one of the bowls and she quickly ate them. She was hungry, (Robin was always hungry); but she could not even think about eating the watery spaghetti. She cleaned the dishes, the stove, the table, and the floor. Then she was asked to put away the children's toys! There were so many and they were spread out all over the room.

"Robin?" The youngest boy was calling.

"Yes JJ."

"Will you marry me?"

"Why?"

"Because you're pretty."

"Well, alright. Maybe I will."

"Well come on!"

"I can't yet. First I have to put all of these toys away."

"When you finish?"

"Yeah, when I'm finished." Robin said as she continued picking up the toys and stuffing them into the storage chest. JJ helped to put away the toys. Once the room was straightened up Robin kept her promise to play marriage, but to Robin's surprise JJ was being too grown for the play.

"I'm going to work Honey," he said.

"Bye," said Robin.

"You don't say bye, you say 'alright honey' and you give me a kiss."

"I'll say 'alright honey' but I'm not giving you a kiss."

"Why not; my mommy kisses my daddy goodbye".

"They are married for real, we are just playing and I am not allowed to kiss boys."

"Oh boy." JJ said, obviously disappointed. "Okay maybe tomorrow," he said as he ran to go play with his siblings.

Robin went to where Mrs. James was and collected $2 for the work she had done. As she went to put the money in her pocket she touched her Aunt Nita's change and remembered that she was supposed to have gone to the store over an hour ago! She ran up the street and around the corner and hurried back with Nita's stuff.

"Where have you been?" Nita asked as she pushed her back coming through the door.

"I'm sorry, I forgot."

"How you forgot?" Nita said grabbing the bag from her hand. "Well I just forgot to pay you. How about that." She said as she pushed Robin upside the head and tried to walk away. Robin jumped in front of her.

"No! How about you give me my dime right now," she demanded.

"I'm not giving you anything because you should have gone and came back. You didn't so you don't get paid."

Robin was seething! She knew not to trust her aunt, but she did not want to fight her. She would wait, there would be another time. She would get her dime!

"Bunk you, you fat heifer," Robin said as she decided to leave again!

Two whole dollars, she hadn't had that much money since about a month ago. She went to "Farmingdales" down the block across Jackson Avenue. She smiled a sad smile as she thought about how it came to be that she had learned how to cross that street...

In the store she brought a pound of ground beef .35 cents, 1 small onion .3 cents, a loaf of bread .29 cents, and two pounds of potatoes .20 cents. She added a pack of Kool-aid .05 cents for a total of .92 cents spent. What a treat for her sisters and she had money left over. She went across to Champs candy store and bought some two for a penny candy and cookies. When she got back to the house she mashed and mixed the meat with the onion she had chopped up; just like her mother had taught her. She looked and saw that there were some eggs so she went and asked her grandmother if she could have one? Her grandmother said "yes" and Robin added it to the meat mixture with a lot of salt and pepper for flavor. She peeled and cut the potatoes into strips. She let the potatoes sit in salted water while she made the burgers. She cooked the burgers nice and slow; planning to "fry" the French fries in the grease that came from cooking the burgers. Because she cooked the burgers slowly they soaked in their own fat and were very greasy. Robin didn't care, the bread would soak it up. She sat the little flattened patties to the side and drained her potatoes. She very cautiously put them into the hot grease, fearful of the grease popping her. The potatoes plopped around, cooked and boiled in the animal fat, but they never crisped up. They softened and Robin knew that they had indeed cooked; but they did not "fry" at all! Oh well, they would have to do as done. Just as she was about to go and call her sisters to come and eat the greasy treat Marybelle and Nita came into the kitchen asking about what she had been doing.

"What do you call yourself cooking this time," Marybelle asked?

"Some hamburgers and French Fries." Robin said.

"You cooked enough for everybody?" Marybelle asked.

"I cooked what I had. It's only enough for my sisters and me. I'm sorry."

"You sorry? What if I said I was sorry and didn't feed you and your sisters when I cooked," asked Marybelle?

Robin kept quiet. She was used to this from her grandmother. Her grandmother seemed to enjoy antagonizing and being spiteful towards Robin and her siblings from time to time for some unknown reason or another. Like the time she had Nita rinse off, open, and heat a totally rusted can of super hot tamales; to which she took great pleasure and found great humor, in watching as the starving little girls ate small bites of the over-spiced food. They were so spicey the girls needed to drink water to cool their tongues before taking the next bite. Or the time last Christmas when she slapped Robin in the eye with a stuffed sock for not sleeping and trying to see Santa leave gifts; again finding great humor in her behavior...

"Excuse me, may I go and get my sisters before the potatoes get cold?" Robin asked after a moment or two of silence.

"Go get your sisters, just make sure you clean my kitchen after you finish serving your feast!" Marybelle said as she turned and walked away. Then Nita took one of the burgers and Robin became enraged. She jumped on Nita's back and started yelling, "Put it back, put it back!" Marybelle turned around and grabbed at the two girls and pushed Robin away from Nita. "What the heck is wrong with you girl?" Marybelle asked.

"She took one of our burgers and I want it back, I want it right now!" Robin demanded, steaming mad and ready to fight.

Marybelle turned to her daughter saying "Nita put back their food! What did you take it for? You're not hungry. Now you cut that out," she said as she snatched at Nita by the sleeve of her shirt; and with that Nita tossed the shriveled patty back onto the plate and stuck out her tongue at Robin. Robin stuck her tongue right back out at her, she didn't care.

Her sisters ate through the food like the hungry children that they often were. No one ever cooked as good as their mother used to; but Robin always tried... and she always cooked with love like her mother had told her was "what you do!" Being able to supply some of the meals that the children got was one of the main reasons Robin liked running errands. She knew that her mother would expect her to help take care of herself and her siblings.

Even though Marybelle had five children herself; she had not ever been used to cooking for her children the way Robin's mom had been used to cooking for hers. Marybelle's mother- in- law; who was a domestic, would do a lot of the cooking and/or bring leftovers home often. Robin's mother, on the other hand, would fix Sunday dinners at least two to three times a week, and fried chicken was often on the table. It was Robin's favorite! Robin's mom had been teaching Robin how to cook since she was big enough to talk. Marybelle on the other hand had just her two youngest daughters at home nowadays and they pretty much were used to fending for themselves.

Perhaps no one could blame Marybelle who the children also addressed as "Momma". At 44 years old, she was still a rather young woman who spent her last eight years as a widow. Her home was stuck in another era and so was she. When you entered through the back door to the apartment you stepped right into the kitchen. There was a large wooden table with a mixture of mix and match chairs in the center of the room. The floor was patch covered with old worn out layers of vinyl; and where the floor was bare, the wood was old, dried and splintering. The stove was a huge black kerosene burning monstrosity set off in the furthest corner of the room. Just a feet away from the windows was the ventilation system.

There was a rusting, white metal cabinet to the left of the entry door with no doors. Some of the food was so old, the tin cans were rusting through. Special people and company came through the front door at the other end of the apartment. The apartment was a cold water flat with a water heater next to the kerosene stove. For whatever reason, Marybelle's apartment was one of the last apartments to still operate off of a kerosene stove and the old faded vinyl flooring had long ago peeled in parts from the worn wooden floors exposing withered, dried wood that was often the culprit for the many splinters the girls would catch running and moving about the house barefooted.

The sink that hung on the wall could barely hold dishes for one person, no way the number of dishes used daily by this combined tribe. So, many times there were dishes stacked on the floor waiting to be washed; next to coca cola bottles waiting to be cashed in for a nickel per bottle. But Marybelle rarely cashed them so they just stood around collecting roaches that would stick inside, caught in the last few drops of the sweet flavored soda water that had not been able to drain. This room was used the most because the large kerosene stove was the apartment's main source of heat. There were old newspapers that climbed damn near to the ceiling, piled on top of an old storage trunk, in the kitchen as well. But the rest of the house was just more of the same. Clothes were stacked high on everything in every room. Robin loved exploring throughout the house. She made up stories about some of the stuff she found amongst the clutter, like the huge trunk that held the newspapers. Robin told herself that the trunk was full of buried treasure and one day her grandmother would open it and let her play with all of the fine jewels hidden inside.

Chapter 3

"Robin, Robin wake up!" Marybelle was saying. "Go and get Zachary and Pinky. Tell them Mrs. McMillan is coming today, I forgot to send you yesterday to get them. Hurry now she will be here at 10 o'clock and it's 8:20 now." Robin woke up stretching and trying to get her bearings but Marybelle didn't have time for that. "Hurry now, get dressed and get going. Put on that outfit I left out for you."

"Okay, okay, I hear you Momma, I'm going," Robin said as she took her outfit to the bathroom to wash and change. She went into her world of imagination and told herself that she was on a special mission to save the day. She had to hurry and find special agents Hiney and Faith... She laughed as she burst out of the bathroom and prepared to leave. She stopped in her tracks as she saw her grandmother filling bowls with hot cereal.

"Am I eating before I go?" Robin asked.

"No, stop playing. I told you to hurry. I will save you some for when you get back, I will have some for Pinky and Zachary too. Tell them!"

"Okay, I will. Bye, see you later!" Robin said excitedly as she hurried on her way. She slid down the bannisters and went crashing through the doors, pretending to get away from the bad guys chasing her. Just as she prepared to jump from the top step down to the concrete platform below, Mrs James called out to her, stopping her in mid flight.

"Good morning Robin, you busy?" she said chuckling at the child who was obviously posed for take off.

"No... yes. Good morning Mrs. James," Robin managed to say as she pulled herself to an upright stance. "I have to go and get my brother and sister for Marybelle. Mrs. McMillan is coming."

"Oh, I see,"" said Mrs. James. "Well I may need you to run an errand later if you can. Come see me when she is gone, okay?"

"Okay Mrs. James I will." And with that, Robin flew off of the steps and off of the concrete platform. She took off running as fast as her little legs could carry her.

She ran so fast she didn't even realize how out-of-breath she was until she tried to call Zachary's name and nothing came out. She had to bend over on herself and catch her breath. Finally she was able to call up to him and in her rich deep voice he came to the window just as she was about to call for only the second time.

"I'll be right down," he said.

When he came outside he gave Robin a hug and she held him tight. She always did that to Zachary. It was as if she never saw him and that is what he always said... Zachary was tall and slender, handsome with a quiet, sheepish demeanor most of the time.

"Stop that, you're gonna have people thinking you don't ever see me." Zachary said and they both chuckled at the very familiar words.

"Well I don't." Robin said. "I wish you and Pinky were at the house with us. Anyway Momma said you have to come to the house right now, Mrs. McMillan will be there at 10 o'clock and we have to go and get Pinky."

"Well come with me upstairs for a minute and let me tell my grandfather I am leaving. Zachary's grandfather lived in a very modern building. There were two sets of steps between each floor and the banisters were skinny and made of wrought iron. Robin quietly followed Zachary up to the second floor and as they entered the apartment they walked right into the kitchen/dining area.

Did you eat?" Zachary asked.

"No, not yet. Marybelle told me to tell you both that she will have some hot cereal left for us and that we have to hurry."

"Okay. Would you like a piece of buttered roll? I'm gonna have some." Zachary said. "Don't worry, we got time."

"Alright" Robin said as she let her big brother make her a buttered roll. His Grandfather came out the back room in pajamas and a robe, old and leaning over, just what Robin pictured a Grandfather to look like, except with clothes instead of PJ's.

"Good morning Mr. Johnston," Robin said to the old man.

"Good morning Little Miss. What on earth has you up and about so early this day?"

"She came to get me because the social worker is coming today. So I'm gonna go and I will be back on the weekend if it's okay with you?"

"Of course it's okay. I told you, you are welcomed here any time. I'm just sorry the place isn't big enough so I can keep you all the time. Speaking of which, I see that you folded up the bed coverings and left them on the couch. Good job, don't worry about putting them away. I will take care of it."

With that Robin and Zachary walked with their buttered rolls plus he took one for Pinky. Zachary's grandpa worked in a bakery and kept day old rolls and breads around. Robin felt that time was getting away from them and wanted to run to where Pinky was but Zachary didn't feel like running, nor was he worried about the time. They were all taught to mind their manners and to listen and respect their elders, but Zachary and Pinky just seemed to have their ways about them when it came to their grandmother. Neither one ever wanted to be there. They both preferred staying from place to place and so; they just did. Marybelle just required of them that every now and then they should stop by and tell her where they were going to be; just in case she ever needed them for anything, like today. For some reason or another, that Robin was never clear about, Marybelle always wanted Mrs. McMillan to believe that Pinky and Zachary stayed in the overcrowded house with the rest of the children. The truth was, they hardly ever slept in her house anymore. If it wasn't for the girls, they might never even go by her house. When they got to Kay-Kay's house where Pinky was staying, Robin called out in her deep rich voice again, but this time she called three times before Pinky came tumbling out of a window on the side of the building.

"Hey! Keep quiet! Everybody is asleep. What are you trying to do, get me kicked out?" Pinky asked in whispered tones. Robin was embarrassed.

"So what's up? What Marybelle wants now?" Pinky asked.

"Mrs. McMillan is coming at 10." Zachary said.

"Should have known." Pinky said.

"Yeah, as much as she needs us, you would think she would give some of that money to us, just for showing up." Zachary said.

Robin just stood there looking dumbfounded. She never knew what these two were talking about or scheming when they were together. "What money?" she asked.

"The welfare check she gets to take care of y'all. I know you don't think she keeps y'all because she is just such a loving grandmother, right?" said Pinky sarcastically.

"No. She doesn't know about stuff like that." said Zachary with compassion for his little sister.

"Well look here," Pinky said, "every month Marybelle

gets a check for taking care of us, only thing is, she don't hardly take care of us. She acts like we are a problem. Does she ever make you feel like she cares about you?"

"No," Robin said quietly.

"Well if you ask me, it's because she doesn't," said Pinky. As they started back toward their grandmother's house.

"It's not that she doesn't care, it's more like she doesn't know how to," said Zachary. "We are a lot of kids. Maybe that is just too much for one person to have to take care of. Heck, I know my grandfather loves me, but he can't even take care of just me!" as he handed Pinky her buttered roll.

"Thank you! It's not about taking care of us as much as it's about; talk to us, play with us, and yes, every now and then feed us. She can do that, she just doesn't want to. She makes me sick!" Pinky said as she spat on the ground.

"Uh!" Robin gasped, knowing Dorothy would be so disappointed in them right now. "Pinky, you know not to talk like that. What about Dorothy, what would she say, what would she think?"

"She would probably think it's about time, we get tired of this old battle-ax!" Pinky replied.

Robin, full of shame and fear, stopped talking and walking. She stood still and just started crying. Loudly! She could hardly be consoled; even as Zachary hugged her and tried to shush her into quietness.

"I want Dorothy, I'm tired too!" she cried in between sobs. "I can't take it either, I hate Nita, she always starting with me and lying. I want to go home."

Then Pinky took her into her arms and rubbed her head. "Come on now, don't cry. I'm sorry, I won't say those kinds of things anymore. Don't cry, come on. Please, stop crying, for me. Please?" And with Pinky's pleading Robin began to calm herself and to finally stop crying.

And as they started on their walk again, Pinky put her arm around Robin's neck, pulling her close and asked, "By the way, what do you mean Nita keeps picking on you and lying on you? You didn't tell me that. I thought I told you if she messed with any of y'all you were to tell me."

"Yes, I know," said Robin "I just wanted to handle her myself. I'm a big girl now too. Just sometimes I can't do anything. Marybelle believes everything she says."

As they were entering the building Pinky turned Robin around to her and said, "I'm sorry for making you cry. I love you, and don't worry about Nita. Her day will come, really soon. You will see."

"It's okay Pinky, you didn't make me cry. I don't even know why I cried, but it wasn't because of you. I love you too, and don't worry about Nita, I'm not afraid of her anymore. You will see!" With that they hugged and all three of them hurried upstairs and into the house.

"Oh good you all made it," said Marybelle as the children all came rushing into the house out of breath from racing up the stairs. "Alright! Take it easy. I wanted you all to hurry but not kill yourselves!"

"Hello Momma," said Zachary.

"Hi Momma," said Robin.

Marybelle and Pinky stared at each other for a moment, neither one saying anything and Marybelle decided it would be best if she just gave in. "Good morning everyone! Zachary and Pinky come here and let me look at you two. Do you want to change?"

"No thank you," Zachary said.

Pinky said, "What you got for me?"

"What do you have for me? Not 'what you got'. Look over there on the sofa. I laid you out an outfit; try it on. It should fit." Pinky picked up the items and examined them then she went into the bathroom and put them on. They were from the second hand clothes pile but surprisingly to Pinky; they looked alright on her. They were knee length (Bermuda) shorts and a short sleeves tie-dye tee shirt.

When Pinky came out of the bathroom she had folded the shorts several times until the cuffs were almost above her thigh.

"Uh-Uhm, excuse me. Please uncuff those pants and wear them as they were meant to be worn; thank you." Marybelle said; making a firm demand. Pinky looked at Marybelle, then Zachary and Robin and finally back at Marybelle and reluctantly she rolled the pants legs back down. Robin smiled.

"Alright, everyone: to the living room and have a seat please."

"Oh! I almost forgot! Y'all go have your cereal. It's on the table. And hurry back into this living room before Mrs. McMillan gets here please!"

They ate quickly and joined their siblings in the living room where they all were sitting pretty waiting for the social worker.

"I don't think I need to remind anybody that you all are not to talk about me with Mrs. McMillan. You are only to answer questions that have to do with you all and your mother, do I make myself clear?"

"Yes! Yes Ma'am!" Came a chorus of replies.

"Good. So Pinky, where have you been lately? Wait! Do I want to know?" Marybelle asked.

"I don't know if you do," came Pinky's reply, to which Marybelle turned her attention to Zachary.

"How is your Aunt Marsha?" Marybelle asked.

"She is well," he replied.

"Well alright then." Marybelle said. "I'm going to go back here and tend to some house chores. You all just sit quietly. I'm sure Mrs. McMillan will be here soon enough."

As soon as she left the room, two year old Dunk got up and ran to Pinky and climbed into her lap, and then Ging-ging ran to Zachary. Not to be left out; Rosalyn, who was always smiling and doing silly things, climbed on Robin's lap and everyone started laughing.

A knock came at the front door and the children scrambled to sit up straight as they knew it was going to be Mrs. McMillan. Marybelle hurried into the room, giving the children a look of disapproval for not having done as told. Then she just as quickly put on her pleasant face and quickly opened the door.

"Good morning Mrs. McMillan, won't you come in."

"Good morning Mrs. Addison," Mrs. McMillan said as she entered into the cramped space that was now the living room/children's bedroom/ play space and storage. "Good morning children!"

"Good morning Mrs. McMillan," said the children; again in unison.

Marybelle showed Mrs. McMillan to a chair that had been brought into the space just for her. To make room for Marybelle, the children went back to sitting on each other's laps, except Rosalyn; she just squatted onto the floor between Pinky and Robin's feet.

"Well children, how are you all getting along? Zachary, how about you?"

"I am well, thank you."

"Faith Jeanette (Pinky), how about you? What are you doing these last few days of summer?"

"I'm good. I like going swimming with my friends and playing in the park."

"Oh that sounds like good summer fun. Do you take your sisters?"

"No!" Marybelle interjected, "I don't allow her to take the girls without me, the children in that municipal pool can be a bit wild you know."

"Oh, I see," said Mrs. McMillan.

"So then we are up to you Robin, what do you do for fun?"

"I play with my sisters. We jump rope and play tag. Sometimes we make mud pies and eat them."

"Oh, 'and eat them', I bet your mouths end up good and dirty afterwards!" she said and Robin laughed.

"Rosalyn, how about you?"

"I do what they do, I do everything," Rosalyn said pointing her finger from one to another of all of the older children, making everyone laugh!

"Well it sounds like everybody is doing well as usual Mrs. Addison. How about you, how are you doing?"

"I'm well, I don't have any complaints. I was wondering though. You all have been promising to get these children a bed for the longest. What's happening with that? Dunk is still wetting the bed, pretty soon there will be a big ole hole in the mattress and everyone will fall through."

"Oh my, we can't have that happen, now can we?" said Mrs. McMillan as she reached out and took Dunk's hand to draw her near. "How are you?"

"Hi, I want to eat some more," said Dunk waving hello as she rested in the fold of Miss McMillan's Arm and with that Marybelle blushed.

"That one is always hungry! Can't keep up with her appetite," said Marybelle, her voice cracking as she tried not to show her embarrassment.

"Well," said Mrs. McMillan, "It is lunch time and I am hungry too. How about we all go for some ice cream?"

"Yay!" the children all shouted in unison.

"Uh, well, uh we/I wasn't prepared for this," murmured Marybelle as she stammered to gain control of the situation.

"Do you foresee a problem Mrs. Addison?" asked Mrs. Mc Millan in a tone of authority.

"No, no, I guess not," said Marybelle as the children eagerly stood, ready to tear out of the apartment.

"Good then. We will go to one of the local diners and we shall return shortly. Everyone ready? Let's go!"

Pinky took Dunk onto her back and Zachary helped Ging-Ging down the two flights, as Rosalyn and Robin darted past everyone and raced to the bottom landing, making so much noise, their grandmother blushed from further embarrassment.

As Robin ran onto the porch Mrs. James asked her if everything was alright. She told her yes, that they were just going out for ice cream and everyone was so excited. Mrs. James asked her would she be able to run that errand when she got back. She said she would stop by when she got back and they would see. Robin was just so happy to be like a little kid for the moment. They all were!

Mrs. McMillan loaded the 6 children into the State branded car and drove the 8 or so blocks to a place called Larsen's Diner located on Bergen Avenue near Communipaw. Once they were all seated inside she asked if anyone was hungry or did everyone just want ice cream. Only Dunk and Ging-Ging "just wanted ice cream." Everyone else wanted cheeseburgers and fries "too!" So Mrs. McMillan ordered cheeseburgers and fries all around, she herself ordered a turkey club sandwich with a cola, and "hold the fries".

As they waited for their order Mrs. McMillan gently encouraged the children to open up and let down their guards. She had a sense of what they were going through, if they were going through anything at all.

"So Zachary how do you get along in a house with so many girls and no other guys?" she asked.

"I do alright I guess. I've been living with 'all girls' all my life."

"I want to go with Zachary," Ging-Ging said.

"You do? Where?" asked Mrs. McMillan.

"To Zachary house, I want to go. I love Zachary."

"Zachary, where does she think your house is?" asked Mrs. McMillan.

Fright flushed the faces of the three oldest children

until out of the blue Rosalyn said, "she thinks Aunt Marsha's house is his house. Sometimes he sleeps there."

"Why?" asked Mrs. McMillan, of anyone who could give an answer at this point.

"Because Aunt Marsha has a lot of boys," said Pinky.

"I spend the night sometimes too. She has a daughter," said Robin.

"Yeah, our mother had all girls and just me. Aunt Marsha had all boys and one girl," Zachary said adding laughter that broke the mounting tension.

"Oh, I see," said Mrs. McMillan cautiously, "do you all have fun with your grandmother?"

"No, not a lot," said the all too honest Rosalyn. "She doesn't like to play and laugh like our mother does."

Just at that somber moment the cheery waitress came along with the food and the conversation was set aside for the moment.

Everyone ate heartily and with the good table manners that their mother had instilled in them. No talking with food in their mouths, chewing with their mouths closed and asking that something be passed as opposed to reaching across someone's plate. Secretly Mrs. McMillan was surprised to see such good manners and honesty.

"So, about your grandmother; anybody else want to talk about having fun or how you all get along? Faith, what about you?"

"No! I don't want to talk about her. She is my grandmother, that's all. I want to talk about my mother. I miss my mother. I miss her cooking, her playing, I miss talking to her . . .," and with that Pinky started crying and it seemed as though she started a chain reaction as all of the children started crying; saying that they missed their mother too!

Mrs. McMillan moved quickly to try and console the rather large group of children. Once she got Zachary to stop crying he helped to quiet the rest of the children, but

Mrs. McMillan realized that this group was in desperate need of some hope!

"Well, I think I have some good news for you all! It seems as though your mother is well enough to begin having visits with you all, and she desperately wants to see you! So how about I try and arrange for a visit for about a month from now?"

"For real?" asked Pinky.

"Our Mother wants to see us?" asked Zachary.

"We are going to see our mother?" asked Robin.

"Yay! We going to see Dorothy! We going to see Dorothy!" Rosalyn jumped up and started singing and dancing, making everyone laugh!

"Okay, just one thing, please let me be the one to tell your grandmother; and I will not be telling her today. Will everyone please not tell? Can I count on you all?"

"Yes, you can count on us," said Pinky and Zachary.

"Okay, don't tell," said Rosalyn.

"I won't say a word," said Robin.

"Dorothy!" said Ging-Ging.

"Doorthy!" clapped Dunk.

Well maybe Mrs. McMillan will have to hurry and tell after all, thought Robin! As they all laughed at Dunk's show of approval, but at 3 1/2 years old everyone had to wonder if Dunk even remembered her mother.

All and all it was a great outing. Robin was elated as they all came back to the house. Mrs. McMillan let them all out of the car; reminding them to not say a word! She was going to arrange a visit.

Chapter 4

It was now 2:15. It had been a long day so far but Robin kept her word and went and saw Mrs. James. "Hi Mrs. James we are back," she said as she peeped into the screened window and saw Mrs. James lounging on her chaise. "Do you want me to come in?"

"Yes, please!," Mrs. James said as she got up and opened the door and busied herself finding a pen and a piece of paper. "I need you to go to my friend's house and bring me back a package that he has for me. You will have to ride the bus. Do you know how to do that?"

"I've been on the bus before, just never by myself."

"Well do you know where Dwight Street is? Have you ever been there?"

"I don't know the name, so I don't know if I've ever been there."

"Okay, well I will just write everything down," she said as she started writing. When she finished she gave Robin two pieces of paper and told her, "You are going up on the hill to Ocean Avenue near Dwight Street. The address is written here and you just give this note to the bus driver. My friend's name is Mr. Collins. He is going to give you an envelope and you must put it in your pocket and bring it straight back to me, no playing alright?"

"Alright Ma'am, 'no playing'!"

"Here you go, this is your bus fare to get there and Mr. Collins will give you bus fare to get back."

Robin, of course did not tell her grandmother that she was leaving because, as long as she stayed gone until it was time to go to bed, all was well. She had never gone on the bus alone before, nor had she ever run this type of errand. She was feeling like such a big girl right now. Robin was surprised to see the bus stop and let her on. She put her money in the coin box as she gave the bus driver the note. She listened and appreciated the clanking sounds the coinbox made as it turned and churned her coins and everybody else's as they got on all along the route. As she sat up front where the driver pointed her to, she laughed in her head to notice that her feet swung as they hung high above the floor while she sat like a short person on the bus seat. Finally the driver called her forward and pointed to her to walk back one block and down to the next block which would be Ocean Ave. When Robin got off the bus she took a moment to look around to try and get her bearings, but she didn't know where she was, and furthermore, she didn't know where she was going. As she looked around while walking quickly she thought to herself there are a lot of people just out and about. Everybody was laughing and/or talking, singing and/or playing, just doing something; enjoying the summer day's sunshine and heat.

She went down the street like she thought the bus driver said but when she came to the next street it did not say "Ocean" Avenue. So she kept going until she came to the next street, and then the next one; which read Garfield Avenue, and that was a dead end. As she started back towards the direction she had come from, walking up Fulton Avenue, she noticed a group of children playing across the street. She barely passed them and one of them called out to her, "Hey! You! Hey you! Girl! You can't hear?"

Then they were right up on her, and Robin had to respond. "Excuse me?" She asked, puzzled.

"*Excuse you? You excused! What's your name?*"

"My name is Robin, what's yours?"

"My name is Puddintane, ask me again and I'll tell you the same!" to which all of the girl's friends started laughing loudly.

"Putting what?" Robin asked.

"Puddintane! What you doing around here? Where you going?"

"I'm on my way to my uncle's house, so if you will excuse me I have to go!" Robin said as she proceeded to walk away.

"'*You have to go? Why? You in a hurry? You got any money?*" Puddintane was asking as she was holding Robin at bay and pushing her towards the center of the crowd of children. Suddenly she and her friends began feeling all over Robin really quickly; patting her down to see if she had money on her. One of them, a knotty head little boy snatched at Robin's private parts and made Robin feel really afraid! Robin started screaming at the top of her lungs like her mother had taught her. Sure enough a middle aged woman came over to the tight circle and somehow managed to get to the middle and hold on to Robin's arm, "What's going on here?" The woman yelled as she pulled Robin from the crowd and next to her side. The ruffians started to back away. "Oh nothing. She was trying to start some trouble with us." Puddintane lied.

"No I wasn't!" Robin protested. "I'm just trying to get to my uncle's house." And with that the woman told the others "Get on out of here for I beat your behinds and take you home to your mothers!" With that, the children all took off running!

"As for you, where does your uncle live," the nice lady turned to Robin and asked?

"He lives on Ocean Avenue, at 463," said Robin.

"Well, that's Ocean right there!" The lady said, pointing to the corner, just footsteps away. Robin was puzzled; trying to figure out how she had passed it by.

"Do you want me to walk with you?"

"No Ma'am. No thank you. I'm alright now. Thank you!"

"You are welcome, but you better hurry up and get to where you are going. It will be dark soon." With that, it was now Robin's turn to take off running, and run she did. Now she was looking for 463 and she did not see it. But she did notice that it was starting to get dark out and what had seemed nice, lively and inviting earlier, was now beginning to sound and look like a scary, horror show. The sounds of children playing were now replaced by guys playing dice and "shooby-doo-ing" in doorways. Cars screeched every now and then as people crossed the busy two-lane road without care or notice. Robin just wanted to get home. "Hey little girl! Are you okay?", asked a man.

"No! I'm lost! I can't find my uncle's house," said Robin anxiously.

"Well where does he live?"

"463 Ocean."

"Oh, that's right there," said the gentleman, pointing to a house two doors away with a set of very steep steps.

"Do you want me to go with you?," he asked.

"No. No, thank you." Robin said, as she ran over to the house and up the steps; still not seeing a number on the house or its door. She rang the doorbell and then noticed that the man who had helped her was still watching her. A big, tall, burley man opened the door rather quickly and, looking down at her asked, "Are you Robin? What took you so long?"

"Yes. I was lost!" Robin said as he brought her into the vestibule and closed the door behind her.

"Oh! You poor thing. And you are so tiny."

"I'm seven! I'm going to be eight soon," Robin said proudly.

"Oh! Eight. I see. That is certainly a big girl's number!," Mr. Collins said laughing. "Here now, put this in your pocket," he said as he gave her the envelope. "This is your bus fare to get back," he said as he handed her some loose coins. "You can just catch the Ocean Avenue bus and get off on Ege. That should be easier." As he went to open the door to let her out, Robin blurted out, "I'm scared!"

"Oh, alright, how about I put you on the bus. Will that help?"

"Yes!" Robin said relieved, and at the same time, ashamed she was afraid.

"Give me just a moment. Let me get my house keys."

After they crossed the street Mr. Collins showed Robin into a store where he bought himself a container of Sealtest milk and the daily paper. He told Robin, "Buy yourself something with your bus fare, I will take care of it;'" and Robin did! She brought 10 cents worth of candy coins (20 pieces), 5 cents worth of two for a penny butter cookies, 5 Bazooka bubble gums for a penny each, 5 one cent Mary Jane's and a bag of potato chips (10c). Mr. Collins and Robin then waited about seven to ten minutes before the Ocean Avenue bus arrived. When it came, it turned out that Mr. Collins knew the driver and told him that Robin was his niece. He asked the bus driver to please put her off the bus at Ege Avenue. Robin wanted to hug him for being so kind but she just said, "Thank you "Uncle!," instead. He laughed and said, "Be careful! Hurry home!" Robin once again sat up front where the driver instructed her to sit, opened and ate her potato chips with great delight. Once they were gone she started on her candy coins only managing to finish four before the driver signaled her to get off. Once she was off the bus, she took a look around through the dusk sky, and she smiled. She knew exactly where she was and she was only too eager to get home! As she was crossing

Jackson Avenue someone snuck up behind her and grabbed her by her sides; scaring the heck out of her. It was Pinky!

"What you doing out here?! Where you coming from?!"

Robin was only too anxious to tell someone, and she was happy it was Pinky. "I was on Ocean and Dwight! I ran an errand for Mrs. James. Her friend Mr. Collins told the bus driver that I was his niece and he let me ride without paying. I brought candy with my bus fare! You want some?" said Robin, holding out some candy coins for Pinky to take. Pinky took the bag instead.

"What did he give you?," Pinky asked.

"Who? What?"

"The package, what was it?"

"An envelope."

"What's in it? I bet you it's money. Where it's at?"

"I don't know what's in it and I don't care."

"Ah, come on give me the envelope, I just want to see it!"

So Robin pulled the envelope out of her pocket and gave it to her big sister.

"See! It is money!," said Pinky, "I told you. Let's open it!"

"No, we won't!", Robin said as she snatched the envelope from Pinky and put it back in her own pocket.

"I should have known," said Pinky.

"How do I look letting you open and steal something from someone who I am working for?"

"Well she wouldn't blame you if someone *stole* it from you."

"Maybe she wouldn't but you are not gonna steal from me, and some kids already tried to steal from me today. They made me mad and they scared me."

"What?! What you mean somebody tried to steal from you?! Who?! Where?! When?!" Pinky's whole demeanor changed with this news. Her antennas went up and she was ready to hurt somebody. She really took her job about protecting her sisters, her family, and her friends very seriously.

"What happened?! I want you to tell me *everything!*" And Robin did . . .

By now they were in front of their door. "You coming up?" Robin asked Pinky.

"No. Not tonight. I'm gonna stay with Sarah and Theresa. I'm coming for you tomorrow and we are going to go and teach those kids a lesson. No one is going to mess with you! *NO ONE!*"

"It's alright. I'm okay and I don't care. I don't want to teach them a lesson," Robin said, afraid of what they might do to her and Pinky!

"What you talking about?! It's *not* okay. You can't let people get away with putting their hands on you! And we're going to find them and teach them a lesson. Now that's that! I'm coming for you tomorrow!" With that Pinky handed Robin back her bag and ran down the street. When Robin went to get another candy coin from the bag she realized all she had left were her Mary Jane's and a couple of pieces of Bazooka bubble gum.

Chapter 5

When Robin woke up she looked out the window and saw rain coming down looking hard and cold. It made her realize how tired she was. She did not sleep well at all; fearing Pinky's return and the revisit to "PuddinTane". The rain offered a little relief as she thought to herself "surely we won't have to go". More good feelings came when she remembered how Mrs. James had been so upset at all that she had gone through on her first errand away from home that she gave her $3.50! Robin was so excited she could burst! She woke up her sisters quietly and asked them, "Did anyone tell the "secret" to Marybelle?" They all said no and she started tickling Dunk and Ging-Ging to make sure; and to hear them laugh. Rosalyn, never one to be left out, climbed on Robin's back and started tickling her. Robin fell and begged for mercy!

"Hey what's going on in there? It's too early for all of that ruckus," came their grandmother's voice.

"Sorry Momma, my fault!" Robin yelled back.

"Hey I got something for y'all!" Robin whispered as she passed out the last of the Maryjane's to her sisters. "Okay, keep quiet. I'm gonna fix you all some cereal, then I will come and get y'all, okay."

"Okay Robin," they all said.

As Robin passed through the railroad track rooms

Marybelle stopped her. "What happened to you yesterday? I thought Mrs. McMillan decided to keep you and give you to someone else."

"No, I'm sorry. Mrs. James asked me to run an errand and I did, but I didn't know where I was going so I got lost."

"You got lost? Well where did you go?"

"I went on the bus to Dwight Street," Robin said proudly.

"Dwight Street?! No! You are *not* allowed to go that far away from here without my knowledge or permission! Do you understand?! And I will just have to have a talk with Mrs. James. The nerve of her!"

"Oh, I'm sorry Momma, it was my fault. Please don't say anything to Mrs. James. I won't do that again. Please. I like working for her, she didn't mean any harm," Robin pleaded.

"Alright, alright, calm yourself now. I won't say anything, but I bet never hear of such foolishness again. Your mother will kill me if something happens to anyone of you children. And I'm not about to die over someone else's foolishness. So with all of that, what she give you for your troubles?"

"She gave me $2.50," Robin lied.

"Well that's not bad. Can you buy some bread?"

"Yes Ma'am, but it's raining really hard out, can I get it later?"

"Yes, sure, that's not a problem. What do you plan on buying with your money this time?"

"I don't know Momma. I might just save it."

"Uhm, that sounds like an idea."

"May I go now? I told my sisters I was going to fix their cereal."

"Yes, yes go ahead. Robin when your mother comes for you, I'm gonna tell her how good a girl you've been, how hard you work. Thank you!"

"Thank you Momma! And you are welcome." Robin replied. It felt good to hear her grandmother say that, but it made her curious. She wondered if Mrs. McMillan had told her about Dorothy. Oh well, not to worry, in due time everyone would know and be talking about the visit and she could tell her mother herself about how hard she tried "minding her manners" as she had been taught. "Hard work"? That would be a whole other story.

While Robin was fixing the bowls of corn flakes for her sisters and herself Nita wandered into the kitchen still adjusting to being awake.

"Can you make me a bowl too," she asked?

Just then Valerie was passing through. "You don't think she has enough responsibility fixing bowls for her little sisters? Why can't you fix your own?" Valerie asked.

"Who asked you?" Nita said.

"It's okay Aunt Valerie," Robin said as she pulled one more bowl from the dish rack and started pouring the cereal. "Aunt" Valerie was just a teenager, ten years older than Robin. She was cool though and she never picked on Robin and her sisters, or made them feel like they were not wanted. So Robin liked calling her Aunt and Auntie, and Valerie enjoyed hearing it, except when she was around the "cool boys" on the block. She said then it made her sound like she was old. Plus Robin had another fondness for her Aunt Valerie, she was the only one who came to Dorothy's aid on that awful day.

"Would you like me to make you a bowl Auntie?" Robin asked.

"No thank you Robin. I gotta go. I gotta get to Lucille's house before the rain comes back."

"Come back? It stopped?" Robin asked in a slight, quiet panic.

"Yeah, the sun is trying to come out."

"Oh, okay, I guess we're going to have sunshine after all." Robin said apprehensively.

"Yes, that's why I need to get out of here. Y'all have fun. Momma "I'M OUT!" she yelled as she left the apartment.

"ALRIGHT!" Marybelle yelled back.

With that Robin made her way back through the rooms and called her sisters to come eat. After everyone had finished eating and the table was cleared, Robin washed and dressed Dunk and helped Ging-Ging put on her clothes. As she was now preparing to wash and dress herself, Nita called her attention to the sink full of dishes.

"You know you have to wash these," she whispered softly.

"No! It's your turn," Robin replied.

"No, it's your turn and you are going to have to do them." Nita said a little louder but forcibly.

"It's your turn and I'm not doing anything." With that Robin went into the bathroom, took her bird bath, and put her clothes on. As she came out of the bathroom Marybelle and Nita were standing there discussing the dirty dishes in the sink and on the floor.

"I told her that she needs to get them done but she just said 'Bunk Me'," Nita was saying as Robin entered the kitchen.

"You 'Bunking' people? Nita says it's your turn to do these dishes and I want them done."

"It's not my turn Ma'am, it's Nita's. She was supposed to do them yesterday, but they're still here. I did them the other day," Robin said, rolling her eyes at Nita.

"You see that, she rolled her eyes at me and she is calling me a liar!" Nita blurted out, and with that Marybelle smacked her gently in her mouth. "Watch your mouth! What about it Robin, are you calling Nita a 'liar'?"

"No, Ma'am. I'm not calling her anything. I'm just saying that I did the dishes the other day and today is her turn and she knows it!"

"Momma, she and her sisters use so many dishes, that's why they are always dirty and that's why she thinks she did them, but she didn't. It's her turn!" Nita lied.

"Well, all I know is I want these dishes washed. Robin

you do them today and Nita will do them tomorrow, she doesn't have to lie. You all do make more dirty dishes, so it won't hurt you to do them more often. Get them done!" Marybelle turned and walked away. Robin was fuming! She was so mad she could've punched Nita in the face. Calling someone a liar and punching people in the face was not allowed.

Just as Robin was loading the sink with the last load of dirty pots Pinky came in. Robin looked towards the window and noticed that the sun was in full force; making its presence known. She sighed and just started to cry, in whimpers.

"What's the matter with you?" Pinky asked.

"Nothing!" she sobbed.

"Then why are you over there with the snot face?" Pinky said, attempting to make her smile.

"I don't have a snot face," Robin said as she wiped her nose and face on the sleeve of her shirt, smiling ever so slightly. "Nita did it again, she lied and Marybelle just believed her and now I'm stuck washing her dishes. So I'm not going to be able to go with you?" Robin said, trying not to show the one bright side in all of her current woes.

"What you talking about, you can so go. I will just help you." And with that Pinky took the broom and started sweeping the floor. As they were finishing the last details of the cleanup; Pinky brushing off the stove and Robin wiping the table, Nita came in. A few feet behind her was Marybelle.

"What's up Nita? How you doing?" Pinky asked.

"Nothing, what's up with you," Nita responded, looking puzzled.

"David told me to tell you to come around to the park on Virginia later," Pinky said as if she did not see her grandmother.

"What? Who? Say what?" Nita was stammering to say as

her mother stepped up behind her and slapped her upside the head.

"Who? Who is sending you messages to meet at what park? Let me find you up in some fast behind boy's face and see if I don't break your neck," Marybelle was saying as she was steadily swiping at Nita. Nita was doing her best to block the licks she was receiving; for what she did not know!

Pinky could hardly keep from laughing as she snatched Robin and pulled her out of the house. "Let's go!" she said as she ran down the stairs two at a time with Robin rushing to keep up. When they got down stairs on the porch Robin didn't know if she should go with Pinky or go upstairs and save Nita; and Pinky could tell.

"Ah stop worrying about Nita! I told you I was going to get her! I know she is a liar and a trouble maker and every chance I get I'm gonna start making trouble for her. Now come on, will you? We got some kids to go see." Pinky was 8 going on 29. She was Robin's hero and Robin didn't even know the word. She admired everything her big sister did and to Robin, Pinky could do no wrong. Their mother had taught them all that each one was to take care of the one underneath them, but somehow Pinky and Robin took responsibility for everybody. Robin would think for the family and Pinky would fight. It wasn't by accident that it worked out like that either. By the time the two of them had started school together, Pinky had already been delayed a year. Then, to make matters worse, she was tested and found to have lead poison which affected the way she learned. The doctors had said that it most likely came from the paint chips Pinky used to peel off the wall and eat when she was little. Pinky had wanted Robin to eat the chips too and Robin had tried to eat the 'pretty ice cream' looking chips but she didn't like them because they hurt her teeth. Pinky had strong teeth and didn't seem to bother her. But because of it, Pinky was labeled "slightly retarded. They said she would never learn like the other children. She would not remember if she did learn and she would need a great deal of help to learn. But even at eight it was clear that what she lacked in traditional school book learning, she more than made up for in "street knowledge and awareness!" Pinky was a thinker, a problem solver, and could just as easily connive, scam, and talk or fight her way through many situations. She could think her way through a situation without batting an eye and what she couldn't think through, she would fight through. It was often said that there were grown women in the neighborhood (and some grown boys too) that did not want to have to fight Pinky. Robin, on the other hand, didn't seem to have any common sense. She couldn't even imagine some of the things that Pinky was able to think her way through. The grown up world and experiences weren't yet a part of Robin's frame of reference. But she was always willing to work hard and she never shied away from doing any tasks requested of her; especially if she could get a dollar or two. Everyone called her smart and she could also talk her way in and out of situations. She just preferred to avoid conflicts and fights because she was afraid of anything that seemed violent or complicated. She just always wanted to be nice to everyone all the time. Sometimes that would make Pinky upset, but together they took great care of each other and their siblings. That is all their mother would have expected of them.

As they walked, it seemed as though Pinky was leading them towards the bus stop where Robin had caught the bus yesterday.

"Are we catching the bus?"

"No!" Pinky answered, surprised that Robin would ask that.

"Oh, then where are we going?"

"We're going to get Jenny and Barbara. What you think, we can't go on the Hill and fight just by ourselves."

"Oh! I didn't know you were going to take them." Robin said, feeling a little better about their chances of 'teaching those kids a lesson'.

"You should never go to a fight without your friends. You always want somebody to have your back, or at least be able to tell what happened. You understand?"

"Yes," Robin replied, feeling even more relieved.

At Virginia and Jackson they met up with Jenny and Barbara. "Hey what's up?"

"Nothing much. We ready to do this?" Jenny asked.

"Yeah! Robin tell Jenny everything that happened just like you told me last night."

And Robin did. Just like last night...

Chapter 6

It was a little after 2pm and the girls were only halfway to their destination. "I'm hungry man, I wish I had a dime for some chips." Pinky said.

"I got a dime," said Robin, "I got fifty cents."

"You do?!" asked Jenny excitedly. "Let me get it!" as she held out her hand.

"No! Pinky can have a dime . . ." Robin started to say.

"Give it to her." Pinky was saying, "She is not gonna keep it. In fact, tell us what you want, we'll get it!" Pinky said as she, Jenny, and Barbara slapped each other high fives. So Robin gave them a list of things she would like to have and gave them the fifty cents from her shoe.

"Okay, you wait right there by that mailbox and we will come and get you. Okay?" Pinky said as she nodded. Then she and her friends split up and entered the store separately.

Robin went and waited where she was told to wait. She was nervous as usual and thought that they were taking an awfully long time. Just as she was prepared to walk back to the store she saw them coming. They were laughing and talking loud and eating ice cream! Yes, they had done what they had set out to do. Jenny was eating a milk bar on a stick and Barbara was eating a frozen ice cream sundae. Pinky was finishing biting her way through a cherry red Popsicle when she pulled an ice cream sandwich from under her shirt and handed it to Robin along with another popsicle, some cookie planks, candy coins, and a butter finger. Everything that Robin had asked for they gave her and twenty cents change.

"How did y'all do this?!" Robin asked, totally amazed.

"You don't need to know." Jenny said, "You would only mess around and get somebody caught. You want something or you need something, just tell your sister, or you can tell me," she said as she rubbed Robin on the top of her head.

"Yeah, you just tell me," Pinky said, rubbing her head next.

Robin loved when she was able to hang out with Pinky. They always ended up on something that seemed like the adventures Robin was used to reading about in her fairytale books. Finally, after they were finished with their snacks and had sugar rushes, they were down the street from their destination: their targets.

"Okay Robin, you remember what you have to do?" Pinky asked.

"Yes, I remember." Robin said, scared to death.

"Don't be scared. I'm telling you, they are not going to do anything to you!" Pinky said.

"Yeah, they're not!" Jenny confirmed.

"What if they hit me before you get to them?" Robin asked.

"They won't have time to hit you! We're going to be on them like white on rice, right?" Pinky said turning to Jenny and Barbara.

"Right!" they said in unison.

"Now go ahead!" Pinky urged by pushing her arm forward.

Robin had a long walk up to the middle of the block, and all kinds of thoughts wanted to run through her mind but she wouldn't let them. She trusted Pinky and knew that Pinky trusted Jenny and Barbara so she could trust them too. She was now talking herself into being brave, and it was working. But just for confidence sake she turned and looked back one last time and saw that indeed the girls were right there. In front of her, sure enough, was the group of troublemakers. She took a deep breath and went to walk by just like she had done yesterday, and just like yesterday a voice came from the group calling out, "Hey! Hey you!"

She ignored them, until just like yesterday, they ran up on her and began to surround her.

"Hey! Weren't you here yesterday?" Puddingtane asked, "Did you bring any money this time?" With that they went to try and grab at her. At that very moment Pinky, Jenny, and Barbara (who were sneaking up from behind cars) jumped into the circle. Pinky grabbed Puddingtane and threw her to the ground and started pounding on her face and chest. Jenny grabbed the boy and started wailing on him! Barbara was kicking, grabbing, and windmill swinging at the rest of the children as some tried to disperse and get away. Because the children didn't see Pinky and them coming, the element of surprise worked in the fighting trio's favor!

"Hey come here! Come here!: Pinky was yelling and waving for Robin to come to her. "Hit her! Punch her in the face!" At first, Robin was scared but she knew she had to, so she squatted down and hit the girl softly in the face. "Hit her harder! Hit her like this!" Pinky said as she hit the girl so hard you could hear a cracking sound. So Robin punched her again. Not making quite the same sound, she tried again and again and it began to feel good to Robin, "Good" Pinky was saying, "Good!" Robin then surprised Pinky when she jumped up and went over to where Jenny was still pounding the boy who had touched Robin in her private place. Robin knelt down and punched him a couple of times in *his* stomach and stood up and stomped him in his private place. As he folded and curled from the pain, Robin heard Jenny yell

"Run!" With that Pinky pulled at Robin and they all took off running across Ocean Ave. A block away Pinky grabbed at Robin and they turned up a street. Jenny and Barbara were nowhere to be seen. Holding on to Robin, Pinky crossed them and they ducked in-between two buildings where Pinky let them stop to catch their breath. Pinky tapped Robin on the arm signaling her to follow. They walked out onto another block and headed back up to Jackson Ave. Once there, Pinky busted out laughing and jumping around, throwing air punches in front of Robin. "Yeah that's my girl! That's what I'm *talking* about! You cracked her jaw! She won't be eating right for days!" Pinky said, filled with the pride of victory!

Robin didn't know what to say. She was actually horrified to think someone wouldn't be able to eat. Again Pinky saw the look on her face!

"I'm just kidding, she can eat. But you sure taught her a lesson or two!" At that moment they walked right into Jenny and Barbara; who also gave Robin congratulations for fighting "a good fight!" They were very proud of her. She wanted to be proud too, but she kept thinking about those children having cracked jaws. She didn't even know what a jaw was!

After they dropped Jenny and Barbara off Pinky took her time walking Robin home. She put her arm around her neck. "Hey, what are you gonna tell Dorothy when we see her?" she asked.

"I don't know," Robin said, "I hope she doesn't ask me what we've been doing." Robin said with a grimace.

Pinky laughed. "She *is* going to ask and you can just say 'surviving'. She knows what that is. That's why she went crazy."

"She went crazy for surviving? What is surviving? Stealing and fighting is surviving?" Robin was asking. So many questions swimming in her head and spilling out of her mouth.

"Surviving is living. To live you have to eat and have some place to live. Sometimes you have to fight and steal to eat."

"Dorothy never had to steal. She will beat us for stealing. She told us 'never take something that is not yours' and 'never want what someone else has'. She's gonna kill us for surviving. Watch, you will see. I'm not gonna tell her if she asks me. I'm gonna just have to tell a lie!"

Pinky laughed at Robin, "I love you, you're crazy like your mother. She told you not to lie too, you know that?"

"Yes, I know. It's hard to do everything she told us and not do what she told us not to do!" said Robin.

"Yeah, that's why it's called survival! Now you listen to me: I don't care if you like fighting or not, you now know that you can fight. If anyone messes with you or our sisters, you beat them down just like we just beat down those kids. You hear me? No one has the right to do any old thing they want to you, no one. You understand?"

"Yes, I understand Pinky . . . Pinky am I really crazy?"

Pinky laughed again, "Yes! We *all* are! Now let's get you home."

Robin was perplexed, but she knew that crazy or not she would be alright because she had the coolest, toughest, smartest, sister in the world and together they could make it through anything.

Chapter 7

Finally Mrs. McMillan told Marybelle that the children were going to have a visit with Dorothy. All of a sudden things started to change. Marybelle became more concerned with what the girls were doing, where they were, and whether or not they were enjoying themselves. Pinky told Robin that Marybelle was just worried about what they were going to tell their mother and whether or not Dorothy was going to "get her". Robin laughed to think that a mother could be scared of their child. Dorothy would never be afraid of any of them.

"Robin, don't go anywhere. We have to start doing you and your sister's hair so you can be ready when you go see your mother on Friday. You hear me?" Marybelle called out from the back of the house.

"Okay, yes Ma'am!" Robin called back. Washing their hair, including her own, was always such a chore. Everyone said that she and her sisters had "good hair", but as far as Robin was concerned it was more trouble than it was worth. It was fun to put water and Dixie Peach (or 'Dippity Do' when they had it) on their hair and make ponytails. But when it came to combing through it after washing, it would be just so tangled and nappy. The girls would always wiggle and squirm until Robin just hated helping with washing their hair! Her mother used to just pay someone else to do it but Marybelle would never consider such a thing.

When Marybelle came into the kitchen she asked, "So whose head should we start with first? We will do two today and two tomorrow."

"What about Pinky's?" Robin asked.

"What about hers? You know she won't let anybody do her hair and your mother doesn't expect it. You can do it for her, if she let you, okay?"

"Yes Ma'am, okay!"

"I say we start with Rosalyn. She usually doesn't act up as much," said Marybelle. "ROSALYN," she called "Come here!" Rosalyn came right away, so Robin hurried and took out the four ponytails she had. She brushed and combed through her hair just enough to get her up under the water at the tiny sink. The actual washing was Marybelle's job. Robyn gave Rosalyn a rag, told her to hold it over her eyes, and the washing began. Marybelle pushed and pulled and rubbed the hair like she was washing clothes on her old wash board. Rosalyn moved from side to side and oohed and aahed all over the place. "Stay still!" Marybelle insisted, to no avail. It was hard work washing these girls' heads. As Marybelle was doing the final rinse she told Robin to go get Dunk next.

Robin went to the back room and found Dunk trying to hide by the side of the couch. As Robin took her hand and gently pulled at her, Dunk squirmed and tried to pull away. "No! No! I don't want my hair washed! Please Robin! No!" Dunk started to cry.

"Come on you have to get it washed. Momma said so!"

"No! She's not my Momma! No! I don't want it washed Robin! Please!"

"Come here!" Robin said, grabbing her. "You don't be fresh and mind your manners. You call her Momma and she said you have to. Don't you want your hair to be pretty when we go see Dorothy? I tell you what; if you are good and let Momma wash your hair, I'll give you some of my candy. You want some candy?"

Dunk nodded her head 'yes'.

"Okay, then come on, and remember to be good! Here, I'm gonna give you this one now and I will give you some more when you finish." Robin said as she put a candy coin in Dunk's mouth.

"Thank you!" Dunk said as she let Robin lead her through the house to the kitchen sink. Marybelle pulled up a chair and tapped it, "Come on, get up here." Dunk looked at Robin and climbed up into the torture chamber chair. Robin started drying Rosalyn's hair with the towel and immediately rubbed some hair grease into it so it wouldn't kink up so fast. She had just gotten the first section greased and pulled through when Dunk started giving Marybelle a fit at the sink. "Robin come hold this crazy little girl for I have to whoop her behind." And Robin rushed to assist. She realized that Marybelle had not given Dunk the washcloth to put over her eyes and now they were burning from the shampoo. Robin dried Dunk's face, calmed her down and gave her another candy coin before she had to finish getting her hair washed. Robin had to stand there with her and she helped to hold the cloth over Dunk's eyes.

"Momma, was it hard to do my mother's hair when she was little?" Robin asked.

"No, no I don't think so. But your mother was the oldest, she had to set the example for her brothers and sisters so she couldn't carry on and act up. No, I wasn't having any of that foolishness. Plus your mother was very independent. She liked doing what she had to do to take care of herself."

"You mean like 'survival'?"

"Yes, something like that. Everything wants to survive and most things will do what they have to do to be able to. Look at your little rambunctious sister here," Marybelle was saying, "She thought she was going to die if she had to get this here stuff washed, she was ready to pack and leave," she said as she stuffed Dunk's hair into the towel to pass her off to Robin. "You go on now and finish them up before you get tired! Two down, and two to go!"

"Maybe three!" Robin said, thinking about Pinky!

"Oh yes, maybe three." Marybelle said.

The next morning Marybelle and Robin did the same thing to Ging-Ging and Robin. Ging-Ging had hair that was much thicker than Robin's, Dunk's and Rosalyn's, but it wasn't quite as thick or hard as Pinky's, so it took a bit of work for them to get through the two heads. Robin was a bit tender headed, and it didn't help that Marybelle was not gentle handed when it came to washing their hair. By the time she had finished greasing and pulling through Ging-Ging's hair, her own hair had drawn up into a ball of knots, grease and all. She thought about wetting it and starting again, but she changed her mind. She put some ponytail holders on parted-hair and went to go find Pinky. She bumped into Sarah who told her that Pinky had just left and was headed to the park to catch up with Jenny and Barbara. So she ran to catch up to her.

"PINKY! PINKY!" she called out. She called out once more and Pinky stopped, turned around and saw her.

"What's up, everything alright?" she asked, looking at Robin rather strange.

"Yeah, everything is alright . . . Why are you looking at me like that?"

"Because you look like your hair was in a fight and it lost," she said as she pointed at her hair and started to laugh!

"Yeah, that's why I called you. Can you please come do my hair? Marybelle washed it this morning and it dried too quickly. I don't want her to do it because she hurts our heads. Plus she told me to see if you were going to get your hair washed before you go to see Dorothy. If you want I will do it for you."

"No, no thank you. I don't want you to wash my hair, it's good. It got washed when I was in the pool the other day." Pinky said laughing again. "But I will do yours, come on let's go," and they turned back around.

"What about Jenny and Barbara? Sarah said you were going to meet up with them."

"Yeah, I was. Now they will just have to come and meet up with me. Beat you to the porch!" she said as she tagged Robin and took off running. Robin took off right behind her.

"Let's do your hair out here," Pinky said.

"Okay, I'll go up and get the brush and stuff. I'll be right back."

When Robin came back Pinky was gone! Mrs. James saw her through the window and said, "You looking for Pinky?"

"Yes Ma'am. You seen where she went?"

"Yeah, she left with her two friends a few minutes ago. They walked towards Bergen."

"Oh," said Robin disappointed. She sat down and started sorting out her hair. Man oh man did it hurt! She took one section and put some water on it. Then she held the hair together and started pulling through the nappy cluster of hair with the comb. The whole time squinting her eyes to mask the pain. After a section or two she heard "What are you doing?" from Pinky. As she felt Pinky taking the comb from her hand. "I told you I would do it!"

"You left," said Robin sadly.

"Oh! I just walked Jenny and Barbara to the store on Bergen."

"Where are they?"

"They've gone shopping."

"Shopping? Where?"

"Two Guys."

"Oh that sounds nice, you want to go?"

"No. I'm going tomorrow. I want to see what they gonna get. Alright now get ready." Pinky said as she picked the comb through the nappy section of hair.

"Pinky can you sleep here tonight and until we come from seeing Dorothy?"

"Why, you okay?"

"Yeah, I'm okay but I can't sleep so good. I keep remembering when they came and took Dorothy away. It keeps waking me up and I keep getting scared. I keep thinking they're gonna take her away again and she's gonna leave us standing there."

"Robin, they can't take her away again because she is not here. I get scared too sometimes, but I know that it's not real. They can't do anything else to her or to us."

"To us? What do you mean?"

"To us! They can't take away our mother, they already did. They can't give us to somebody that doesn't love us, they already did. So what else can they do to us? Nothing!"

"So you still think about that day too?"

"Yes, of course, all the time. I remember her waking us up while it was still dark outside and taking us with her" . . .

Chapter 8

"Robin, Pinky wake-up! Get-up!" Dorothy was saying as she shook the girls into wakefulness!

"Huhn? Yes!" Pinky was responding.

"Okay, okay, wake up! I'm up," Robin was mumbling.

Finally the girls were awake enough to hear their mother.

"Yes." The two sleepy little girls were saying, trying to understand what was going on.

"Here, put your clothes on, we have to go." Dorothy said in hushed tones.

The girls looked at each other as they began to put on their clothes, then to their mother. Both too young to know how to make sense of all of the questions trying to form in their young minds.

When they were dressed Dorothy put her fingers to her lips signaling them to keep quiet and follow her.

She quietly opened the front door and stepped into the hallway, waving to the girls to come out with her. Now fully awake, the girls started to think that this was going to be fun and they listened and paid close attention to their mother and her signals. At the steps she did a little victory dance for having gotten this far without notice. She went down the stairs two at a time but quietly and the girls ran down the steps as quietly as they could but fast to keep up with her.

Outside it was still dark as it was early in the a.m. that Dorothy took this adventure. There was no one outside; not near other souls! Dorothy took the girls by the hands and started walking towards Jackson Ave. When she got to the corner she stopped and spoke out loud saying, "I don't think we should." Pinky and Robin looked at each other and up to their mother, who other than holding their hands, didn't seem to pay much attention to them being there.

"Alright, alright. let's go," she was now saying as she made up her mind and crossed Jackson Ave. with the girls in tow. As they came towards the center of the block she leaned down and said to the girls "the trees want me to go with them. I don't want to go with them!"

"The trees?" Robin asked.

"Go where?" Pinky asked.

But Dorothy just kept walking. At times she held the girls' hands tighter, at times she loosened her grip as to almost not hold them at all. At Ocean Avenue the dawn was breaking. Pinky and Robin were surprised to see night turning into day! Pinky pointed to the sky and said "It's daytime!"

"Yeah!" Robin said, hunching her shoulders as if answering and asking if it were. People were coming out now, perhaps on their way to work.

"Hey Dot!" A man in work overalls said, acknowledging Dorothy. "What's going on? Why are you out here so early with your little ladies?" He asked as he winked his eyes at the girls.

"I gotta get them back home. It's not cool to be out here." Dorothy said as she kept moving, not giving the man a chance to stop her movement.

"Oh, okay, do what you gotta do," he said as he watched her hurry on pulling her girls along.

Dorothy turned left onto Ocean Ave. a block or two over she went into a building and knocked on a door. Pinky and Robin knew they were at Ms. Minnie's house. Dorothy knocked and knocked and finally a loud, harsh "Who is it?" came through the door.

"It's me, let me in." Dorothy said in quiet, tired tones.

Ms Minnie quickly removed the chain and lock and swung the door open.

Seeing Dorothy and the girls Ms Minnie hurried and ushered them into the house. "Dorothy what's going on? You alright? Girls are you okay?" Ms Minnie asked, staring down at them.

Pinky hunched her shoulders like she didn't know and Robin shook her head yes, while saying "Yes ma'am!"

So Ms Minnie turned her attention back to Dorothy. "Dot what's going on? Come on, sit down." Dorothy followed Miss Minnie to the sofa and sat on the edge of the corner. Again Miss Minnie asked her what was up? this time Dorothy said "The trees want me to go with them. The strings keep waving to me. They want me to go with them but I don't wanna! I'm tired. I need to go to sleep."

"The trees, strings? Dot what are you talking about? I don't understand? Are you okay?" Ms Minnie was saying, somewhat frantic for the safety of her friend.

"I need to go to sleep." Dorothy said again.

"Okay Dot, lay back and go to sleep. You know you can, It's okay."

"No. I can't! They gone get me if I do. I don't know what to do." Dorothy said, sounding afraid and anxious.

"Dot who's gonna get you? Ms Minnie Asked?

"I don't know? I think they are the keeper of the trees! You know what I'm saying." Dorothy said.

"No Dorothy, I really don't. But if I can help you, You know I will. One thing for sure, ain't nobody coming in this house saying what you can do and what you can't! So, if you want to go to sleep, go on. I will watch the girls." Miss. Minnie said reassuringly.

"Okay, okay, I will," Dorothy said as she slid herself back on the couch. Just as quickly she attempted to get back up and Miss Minnie leaned down towards Dorothy, placing her hands on her shoulders and gently encouraged her to stay still. "It's okay Dorothy. Trust me. It's okay." Dorothy settled back down and it seemed as though she was beginning to get some much needed rest.

Miss Minnie quietly coaxed the girls into her kitchen and quietly offered them some toasted bread with butter and jelly. As they were eating Mr. Richard, Miss Minnie's husband wandered into the kitchen. "Hey, hi girls," he said, giving a heads up nod to the little guest.

"Hi," Pinky and Robin said in response.

"What's going on?" He asked his wife, making another head nod towards the living room.

"I don't know?" Miss Minnie whispered to her husband. "I think something is wrong with Dot. She keeps talking about something wanting her. She is scared and tired. I told her to go ahead and get some rest, but I think something is seriously wrong." Miss Minnie told him.

"Ain't nothing wrong with her that a good stiff drink can't handle," Mr. Richard said, not at all concerned with whispering for the sake of the children. "Give her a drink and tell her to go home. Too damn early in the morning for all this going on." Mr Richard said adamantly.

"Ah come on Honey. Go on, go back to bed. I'll take care of her and be back to bed in just a bit. She got these babies with her and I just want to make sure she is good. Go on, go on now. I'll be there shortly," Miss Minnie said as she gently nudged her husband towards their bedroom.

She then came back and tended to Pinky and Robin who had both finished eating the toast and both were coated with the sticky jelly. Miss Minnie took them to the bathroom and helped them wash their face and hands. As they were coming out of the bathroom, Dorothy was walking towards them. Come here she snarled as she grabbed Robin and pulled her near and held out her hand to Pinky, who grabbed it and nestled close to her mother with a look of fear in her face.

"Dot! How you feeling? You rested?" Miss Minnie was asking.

"Get away," Dorothy was growling. Her body poised in a stance like an animal ready to pounce upon prey.

"Dot! What's wrong? Something is wrong! We need to take you home or call someone," Miss Minnie said, terribly concerned.

Mr. Richard hearing the commotion came to assist his wife.

"Hey Dot, what's going on? How you doing? You need a drink? Let me get you a drink," he said as he moved towards the china cabinet.

Just as he stepped past Dorothy, she hurried to the door, opening it and pushed her girls out. She followed them onto the porch and then took the lead going down the steps quickly. Miss Minnie was on the porch calling out to her.

"Dot go home! Take those girls home." Miss Minnie said.

Mr. Richard came and stood next to her, waving his hand after Dot. "Let her go! Ain't nothing wrong with her. She's just crazy, but no more than usual. Though I ain't never known her to turn down a drink. I ain't never known her to do that! Now that's what's crazy." He said laughing out loud and with that, he put his hand around his wife's waist and showed her back into the house.

From there Dorothy continued her journey, slipping more and more away. Holding the girls' hands really tight, she ran them across Ocean Ave. She was walking fast but seemingly unaware of the traffic as cars stopped and screeched, blowing their horns and calling out to her to "Get out of the street!"

She was now by Arlington Ave Park and she stopped and

walked through. She let go of the girls hands and wandered over to a tree. The girls just watched. Dorothy placed her hand on the tree and leaned in as if she was listening. She lifted her head and started talking as if she was answering questions. Robin and Pinky only a few feet from her and hearing her, started to laugh quietly into their hands. After her mutterings, Dorothy patted the tree and again took the girls by the hands and started on another walk.

In a short time she was at Garfield near Communipaw calling up to a window.

"Rev! Reverend!"

Within seconds a short pudgy man opened the door to the building.

Pinky and Robin knew him as Reverend Hank. "Hey Dot! What's up? Hello girls. Come in! Come on everyone, come in," he said as he stepped to the side and Dorothy ushered the girls in and led them up a flight of stairs into Reverend Hanks house. He closed the door behind him and turned and called "Ev. Evelyn come see who's here!"

From behind a set of heavy draperies hanging across a doorway came a somewhat tall, big boned, beautiful woman. "Hey! Dot! To what do we owe this visit?" Evelyn was asking, walking towards Dorothy with her arms held out to give a hug. Dorothy lifted her hand forbidding the embrace, causing Ev and the Reverend to pause and take notice. Then the Reverend spoke to Pinky and Robin, "How are you girls doing? Are you hungry? Have you eaten?" As soon as he paused, Pinky said "We had toast, but we hungry."

"Good," he said. "Ms Ev is going to fix you all something to eat, can you two go and help her please? I'm gonna talk to your momma for a minute then we will come and join you okay?" He said, nodding to his wife to take the girls.

He showed Dorothy to the dining room and they sat down. "Dot, what's up? What's going on?" He asked.

"I don't know what's going on," Dorothy managed to say.

"I'm hearing things! Trees are calling me; they want me to go with them. Well, not the trees. The strings on the trees. They want me to go with them. What's going on?" Dorothy asked. "I think someone put roots on me! I need you to get them off. I'm scared, man. I'm scared!" Dorothy said as she reached out and gripped his forearm. She started to cry. The Reverend stood up and stepped away for a quick moment coming back just as quickly; he handed Dorothy a handkerchief. She wiped her face and laid the handkerchief on her lap as she continued expressing her concerns. "You think someone put roots on me Rev.?" She asked.

"I don't know Dot. But I don't think so. Why, why would anyone want to do that to you?"

"Yeah, I don't do nothing to hurt nobody. But still why are the trees trying to take me with them? Something is wrong Rev. Something is really wrong," Dorothy said, the most coherent she had been throughout that morning.

"Dot, were you drinking this morning? Do you feel like you need a drink," he asked?

"I don't want no drink and I am not drunk, Rev. I came to you because I thought you would understand. This ain't right what I'm feeling, what I'm thinking. It ain't right, and Rev I'm really, really scared right now," Dorothy said with the fear showing on her face!

"I apologize. I just needed to ask. Would you like me to pray with you?"

"Yes, maybe that will help Rev. Can you pray for me. Can I pray with you," Dorothy asked?

"Yes," he said holding his hands out for her to take. She stood holding his hands and he could feel her nerves as her hands vibrated violently in his. For a moment he wanted to pull his hands free because her energy was so powerful and sporadically discharging like some sort of zap gun. "Heavenly Father, Lord of all Creation; please Lord, help your child! She is crying out for you Dear Lord and you hear her. Please remove whatever is troubling her and give her the comfort she needs. She is praying and asking for your mercy. Please pour it down on her as only you can do, Dear God. This is your child, yet she is a mother with children. She needs your grace, your protection and your Fatherly love, Dear Lord..." The Reverend was saying as he took one hand away from Dorothy and laid it on her forehead.

Dorothy reacted to his touch as she felt something move through her body. Her body swayed back and forth as she gave off the idea that she was about to heave her weight thrown forward. The Reverend freed his hand and caught her as she collapsed in his arms. He helped her to the sofa nearby and she sunk deep into its cushions.

"Ev, Evelyn," he called out cautiously and quietly, but firm enough that Evelyn came quickly; leaving the girls in the kitchen preparing to eat the hot breakfast she was cooking. She saw Dorothy slumped into the couch. She stepped around her husband and went into the bathroom and came back with a wrung out cloth that she shook out and began to wipe Dorothy's forehead with. "She thinks someone has put roots on her. She is exhausted," Reverend Hank explained to Evelyn. I think she needs to go to the hospital. How are the girls doing, poor little babies?"

"They're okay. Smart little girls, they are. I was just about to fix their plates. I thought you were calling me to let me know that Dot wanted one. What do you think, shall we try to feed her?" Evelyn asked.

"I'll ask her. As for me; I'll eat later, if I eat at all," Reverend Hank said, sounding exhausted himself. "I tell you what, whatever is bothering her it is very, very heavy!" He said, wiping his brow with his shirt sleeve.

With those words Dorothy started stirring; she opened her eyes and stared out in front of her as if she was looking at nothing. Just a blank stare. "Dot? Dot, you okay," Rev was asking? "The girls are about to eat; would you like to join them?"

Dorothy didn't move or say anything. She just continued to stare.

"Go feed the girls," Rev said to Evelyn, motioning his hand towards the kitchen. "Let me see what I can do."

He took Dorothy by one hand and put his hand on her forehead as he had done earlier. He began to pray again; as he had done earlier. "Father, Heavenly Grace, we thank you for your intervention. She/we feel your grace and divine intervention happening here! Please we pray, let your will be done. Please remove whatever obstacles are in the path of Dot here; make easy her journey through! Please remove her fears and concerns and assure her of your being! She is asking for your help Father. She is crying out to you! Touch her won't you please, Dear God; touch her in the spirit, touch her in the heart. Clear her mind and spirit, Father God, for only you have the power to do so and only you are worthy to be asked." the Reverend was praying.

"Please Father, please!" Dorothy was heard to say before she pushed the reverend's hand away and wailed a piercing sound! It was so loud that the girls came from the kitchen with horror on their face as they attempted to go to their mother. But Evelyn held on to them as she stared, confused at what was happening too!

The Reverend could see the questioning in his wife's eyes and could only shrug his shoulders as he stepped back from Dot whose body was contorting into different twists and turns as she gave out a grunt then a growl. The Reverend was motioning for Evelyn to take the girls into another room, but Dot motioned for them to come to her as she made her way to the door. Again she was taking off!

The reverend followed her and the girls down the steps as Dot swung open the door and started breathing deeply like she was gasping for air. The girls certainly had no idea what was going on; and now they were beginning to get a little afraid of their mother. The reverend said to Pinky "I'm going to call for help!" If she tries to go anywhere; it needs to be home. Can you take her home?" Pinky had a look of fear plastered on her face but she managed to say "I will try." With that the reverend went to the corner just steps away from him near Communipaw to a pay phone and called for an ambulance. By the time he had finished the call Dot had already had the girls running to keep up with her as she was already back to Arlington Park. This time she just cut through diagonally and ended up on Ocean and Bramhall. Surprisingly she was going back the way she came and she was headed towards home! But her talking to herself was becoming more noticeable and her walking was twice as fast. She only slowed down/paused her walking when she came to the corners of streets that she had to cross the girls across. They have to run to catch her hand as she stepped off the curbs a time or two.

In just a short while Dot was at the corners of Ege and Ocean and Pinky and Robin recognized that they were near home. But when they got to Ege and Jackson everything fell completely apart! Dorothy was in the middle of the street fighting, flailing her arms, and growling like an animal. Robin and Pinky were left on the sidewalk and they did not know what to do. Robin was never so scared in all of her life. She was frozen with fear. Pinky was seemingly calm but very observant. She watched as someone pointed to her and Robin and she heard someone say go get her mother, Mrs Adams as they tried talking to her.

"Dorothy, Dorothy are you alright? Come here, get out the street! Dorothy? Dorothy come here!"

People stopped and stared; some whispered and pointed. After a moment a crowd was gathering and through the small crowd Aunt Valerie came through. Robin was so happy to see her aunt; but her aunt did not see her! Valerie was attempting to get her big sister's attention, but Dorothy did not seem to understand. Dorothy was no longer reachable. Whatever was attempting to lure her in had finally done so!

The police came and encouraged people to move on, go about their business, and make room for the ambulance and medics to come in and do what they had to do! After taking information from Aunt Valerie about Dorothy, the medics tried talking to her, but Dorothy only hissed and growled in response. So the medics decided the best way to handle the situation was to "capture" her. They used two long poles with ropes in them that they threw over her head. The ropes held Dorothy's arms to her side and one of the medics stuck a needle in her upper arm as quickly as he could. Dorothy began to quiet down and the medics worked quickly to put her into a white coat with a lot of strings that they wrapped around her in different directions and tied off. With that they were able to put Dorothy in the ambulance and take her away. Some of Aunt Valerie's friends from the block offered her comfort and walked her up the street to her house. The rest of the crowd had dispersed as quickly as they had gathered; and suddenly it came to Robin's awareness that no one came for her and Pinky! No one thought to take them home. Quietly as a four year old would do, Robin began to think in her limited abilities, of all of the horrible things that could happen if no one remembered to look for her and Pinky. How were they going to get home if there was no one there to cross them across the street? Where would they go? How would they eat? Where was her mother?

And as if Pinky instinctively knew everything Robin was thinking and feeling; Pinky took Robin by the hand, looked both ways at the traffic, and crossed them both safely across the street. She took them back to their grandmother's house...

Chapter 9

"That's what I remember most," Robin was saying, "That you crossed us across that street and got us back to Marybelle's house."

"Yeah. I just knew that's what we needed to do. Get to her house. You are my sister, it's what I was supposed to do!"

"Pinky I don't want to be crazy. I don't even like it when you say that we are. Why are we crazy? We never talked to trees. We never go to people's houses early in the morning and we never cut anybody up! I'm scared of crazy!"

"Well don't be. It's not the kind of crazy like Dorothy is and I know I'm a little crazy like her. I'm okay with that. I don't talk to trees but I ate that paint and now I can't think like other people. I can't learn the way you do and when I fight, I always want to hurt somebody. That's why I say we are crazy. You, you are not really crazy. I just say that because she is our mother. You're too nice and too smart to be crazy anyway. But just remember, she wasn't always crazy. I think Rufus might have made her crazy or something. Maybe she just don't like trees . . . we can ask her when we see her."

"I don't want to ask her, I don't think that would be nice."

"Yeah, maybe you're right. I hope she's finished with

being crazy though. I don't ever want to have to live with anybody else ever again."

"Yeah me neither!" agreed Robin.

Somehow it got real quiet between them and finally Pinky finished and pushed Robin away saying, "All done!"

"Wow, I hardly even felt anything. How I look?"

"You look pretty, silly, how else would I make you look?"

"So? Will you stay the night with us?"

"I can't stay tonight, but tomorrow I will. I promise, okay?"

"Okay. Okay, if you say you will stay tomorrow. I know you will. But why can't you stay, what you got to do?"

"Nothing much, just something. But I tell you what; before I go, come with me," Pinky said as she took the comb and grease and stored them behind the porch; "I want to show you something!"

Pinky took Robin down the street, across Jackson Avenue and a couple of doors away from where they were standing when Dorothy was taken away. As Pinky was leading her, Robin slowed down and looked behind her as if she were watching the whole scene play out in her head all over again. That happened to her from time to time, especially times like right now, where Pinky is taking charge, teaching, or showing her something. Then Pinky pulled her into the vestibule of a store front and through a door that led up a narrow stairwell. At the top of the stairs they walked into a brightly painted room with hardly anything in it. There were just a few wooden folding chairs spread about and a big heavy table draped with a table cloth and plastic covering. In the center was an artificial flower arrangement, a plate with some cookies on it, some paper cups, and a metal pitcher half filled with milk. On the wall above the table was a huge wooden cross with a statue of Jesus Christ nailed to it. Pinky poured some milk for Robin and herself and took two cookies telling Robin to help herself. Robin took two cookies too.

"What is this place?" she asked Pinky.

"It's like a house church," Pinky said. "I come here sometimes when I'm tired and when I'm scared."

"You do?" Robin asked, not able to hide her surprise. "You get scared, I never knew that. I don't know why I never knew that."

"You never knew that because I don't let anybody know that. I'm tough. I'm not supposed to get scared. That's how people think, even grown ones. Everybody gets scared sometimes."

"So why do you come here?"

"I don't know. I just do. I do remember that Dorothy brought me here with her a couple of times. But I think I just come here because nobody bothers me. I come, I go. I talk to Jesus and God. I tell them about some of the things I do and still I can come here. They never get mad at me or make the thunder come! Remember what Dorothy used to say?"

"Yeah, she said that the thunder is God being angry, and we had to cover the mirrors and windows and wait until he was through. Yeah, I remember."

"I hear that that's not the truth, that God is not angry. I also was outside when it was thundering and he didn't get me."

"Oh!" said Robin, who would hide under the bed whenever there was thunder. "I don't know about that, it sounds pretty angry to me!"

Pinky took Robin by the hand and led her over to a place where they could kneel and pray. "Pray with me," she said, and she started "Our Father who art in heaven, hallowed be thy name, thy kingdom come. Thy will be done on earth as it is in heaven,"

"Give us this day our daily bread . . ." Robin joined in.

As they finished and went to stand up, Pinky got excited and pulled Robin towards a woman who had been standing in the room quietly watching them.

"Hello Faith! Who is this you have brought with you today?"

"Hi Sister Christine. This is my sister Robin. I told you about her, remember?"

"Yes, I do! Hello Sister Robin, how are you today?"

"No I'm not 'Sister'. Hi I'm her sister," Robin found herself trying to explain.

Pinky and Sister Christine smiled! "She is playing with you", Pinky whispered to Robin.

"Oh!" Robin said blushing for not knowing. "Your name is spelled like Jesus Christ's name," Robin said.

"Why yes! The first half of my name is spelled just like his," Sister Christine said nodding her head towards the cross. "She is smart, just like you said," the Sister said as she turned towards "Faith". Pinky smiled proudly and Robin blushed even more.

"I shall leave you two to do what you were doing as I have to clean and prepare to go. Enjoy your stay, and 'Sister' Robin do come join us again! Bye Faith," said Sister Christine.

This time Robin caught on and she smiled, they all did!

"Good Bye Sister Christine," said Pinky and Robin.

They too had to leave as Pinky had someplace she wanted to go. It drove Robin crazy for real that she would not tell her where!

Chapter 10

The next day Robin was outside with the girls and some other children from the block playing 1-2-3 Red Light. She was the red light of course. As she was turning and calling out 1-2-3 Red Light, she heard Dunk and Ging-Ging break away and run past her with Rosalyn right behind them. She turned to see them all running towards Pinky, extra excited to see her, and she immediately saw why. Pinky had gotten her hair done. It was pressed and curled and it looked good. She looked like the spitting image of their mother!

"Hey what's going on here? You look beautiful. You look like Dorothy." Robin said.

"Yeah that's what Ms. Eloise and Gloria said." They were Jenny's Mother and sister.

"Who did that?" Robin asked, nodding towards Pinky's hairdo.

"Gloria!"

"When?"

"Last night, that's why I couldn't stay. That's why I didn't want you or Marybelle to do my hair. She had **been** promised to do it when it was time."

"Well she did a great job! Where are you on your way too?"

"Nowhere yet, but later I'm still going to Two Guys. I want something nice to wear."

"Yeah, Marybelle said she got our clothes ready but she didn't let me see them yet. I hope they fit."

"Don't worry she might not have 'new clothes' for y'all, but she is not going to send y'all to see Dorothy looking just any old kind of way. She is not going to do that."

"Yeah, I bet you are right," Robin said.

"I'm waiting for Jenny and Barbara, but I'm gonna let you get back to playing 'Red Light', for they get both of us." Pinky said, watching the mayhem about to happen to the children with no light for guidance.

Finally, after Robin was all pooped out, she let her sisters run off to play with the other children behind the back of the house; as they were used to doing whenever she didn't have time to play with them.

As Robin sat on the porch with Pinky she felt like she needed another one of their adventures!

"Hey Pinky, I want to go with you to Two Guys! May I?"

"No you may not, 'Mother May I?'! You may take two steps back and stay here with Dunk and Ging-Ging!"

"Ah come on! Please? Please? Please?!" she begged.

"I'm telling you no, because I know Jenny and Barbara are going to say no! And this time I can't help you. We are going shopping with no money and it's not like hair bows and ice cream sandwiches, it's big time. If we mess up, we go to jail, you understand?"

"Yeah I understand, but you all never mess up, so I still want to go! Besides, you're not going to let anything stop you from seeing Dorothy and neither would I."

"Yeah, you're right about that. Okay, let's see what the girls have to say. But don't get your hopes up," Pinky warned. "I gotta go to the bathroom. I'll be right back. And I'll see if Marybelle has laid out our clothes." With that Pinky took off up the steps.

Soon after Pinky left, Jenny and Barbara came in front of the stoop. "Hi Robin! You seen Pinky?" Jenny asked.

"Hi Jenny! Hi Barbara! Yeah, she just went to use the bathroom. She'll be right back."

"Wow, so y'all going to see Dorothy? You're happy about that I bet!" Jenny said.

"Yeah, we all are, even Pinky. She doesn't get happy a lot!" said Robin.

The girls all laughed!

"Jenny, can I go with y'all to Two Guys please? I want to get something nice to wear too. I can be the lookout again, please? Pinky said only if you and Barbara say yes," Robin pleaded.

"Robin, it's not like the other times. It's a much bigger store and they take children to jail if they get caught. What you gonna do if you get caught?"

"I'm not gonna get caught. I'm only gonna do what Pinky and you two tell me to do. You are not gonna get caught, you never do."

"That's because I know what to do. Pinky and Barbara know what to do. You don't!"

"So tell me then, please," Robin pleaded. "Where did you get that nice coat? Did you get that yesterday?"

"Yes. It's called a windbreaker. How we got it was Barbara's mother gave her some money to buy some clothes. When she came out with the receipt I went back in and got the same things just in different colors. I put them on right there in the store and walked out. If someone would have questioned me, I would have shown them my receipt."

"But no one questioned you right?"

"Right! And today we're going back to get Pinky the same things. If we take you we have to come out and go back in. We only have one receipt! I think you better stay here this time." Jenny said.

"Okay!" Robin said sadly.

Pinky was now coming down the steps. "Hey Jenny! Hey Barbara!"

"Hey Pinky!" they responded.

"It's okay Pinky, I asked her and she said 'not this time'" Robin told Pinky, still sad.

"Oh okay . . . Hey! I'll see if I can bring you something back, I saw the clothes." Pinky said as she was walking away behind the girls.

The girls walked away. After a few minutes Pinky came back and called Robin, "Come on! You can go!" she said. Robin jumped off the porch and ran so fast she nearly fell over herself.

"Whoa!" Jenny said, "You can't be clumsy. Pinky said you're gonna need some new clothes, so we have to take you. You better do everything we say. If you don't you won't ever go with us again. You understand?"

"Yes, yes! I understand! I will!" Robin gushed, reassuringly.

So the girls went down the back streets crossing the boulevard, down to Westside Ave. and further still; across route 440. Robin thought it was a long way away from home and she was afraid of the highway. But she tried not to show it. Pinky must have sensed it because she told her "Come on!" as she grabbed her hand and held it tight. They got across the highway nice and safe, and Robin started to relax a little; until they entered the store that is. The store was huge. Robin never saw anything like it. There were people everywhere and none of them were walking up to little girls asking if they were alright. Panic started to set in, but none of the girls noticed. They were fixed on their mission. They all headed over to the children's clothes. Immediately Pinky found the windbreaker she wanted and put it on.

"What color do you want? Get it and put it on. Hurry up!" she said to Robin without looking at her. Had she looked she would have noticed that Robin was stricken with panic! Just then Jenny dropped a pair of white sneakers by Pinky's feet.

"Here these should fit, try them on," she said, already popping the string that held them together. They were a perfect fit. Just then everybody took notice of Robin, who still had not tried on the windbreaker.

"Ah damn!" Jenny said as she noticed the panic in the 'little' girl's eyes. "She's about to lose it Pinky! Here, take this receipt. We are out of here. I told you: she's your sister, she's your problem!" With that Jenny and Barbara just walked away and out through the automatic doors.

"Robin! Robin, you listening to me!?" Pinky was asking.

"Yes, I'm listening," Robin managed to respond, sounding as if she were hypnotized.

"Okay, I have my outfit on. We can just leave. You want to just leave?"

"Yeah . . . No! No I want an outfit too," came Robin's response.

"Okay, all you have to do is put on the coat, like I did. Then we can go over and you can put on some sneakers. You want to?"

"Yes! I want to but I'm scared!"

"Well, you can't be scared, you gotta just do it. You said you would do whatever I told you to do, right? Ain't that what you said?" Pinky challenged; feeling somewhat annoyed and being very impatient.

"Yeah, that's what I said. I want to, but . . ."

"No 'but's' Robin! Either you gonna do it or we gotta go!"

"Okay . . ." Robin said hesitantly, as she took a blue windbreaker off the rack and tried it on.

"Yeah, see, that's nice. Okay now we have to take the tags off," Pinky said as she popped them off the coat. "Now, let's go get the sneakers. I can't guess what size you're gonna fit so you're gonna have to try them on."

"No, wait Pinky, I don't want blue. I want the orange one," Robin said, obviously feeling more into it.

"What? No! You have to keep the blue one. I already popped the tags. Let's go get the sneakers! Come on!" Pinky said as she walked away and Robin followed behind her.

When they started trying on the sneakers Robin was much more relaxed. Pinky looked up and saw that Jenny and Barbara had come back into the store and were headed over to them. Just at that moment, as soon as she had popped the string holding the sneakers together, the in-store security officer was walking up to her. Jenny and Barbara did a quick about face and walked back out. Robin thought the security officer was a police officer.

"Pinky, Pinky!" Robin said in a panic stricken tone.

"I know, I see him!" Pinky responded in aggravation.

"Do you two need any help?" the security guard asked.

"No thank you. We just want to try these on to see what size she wears," said Pinky.

"Well you know, you are not supposed to pop the string until you buy them. That's how people know that they are for sale."

"Oh, we didn't know that. Sorry," Pinky said.

"Yes, we're sorry," Robin managed to say.

"Who are you here with? Where are your parents?" the security guard asked.

"Our mother's not here, she's in the hospital," Pinky said.

"Oh, I'm sorry to hear that, I wish her well. So who are you here with?" he asked again. Robin looked at Pinky hoping she knew what to say. Pinky didn't.

"Okay young ladies, perhaps you want to come with me," the security guard said, taking Pinky by the shoulder and Robin walking in a tight lockstep right next to her. The security guard was taking them to an office in the back, which Robin thought was the jail.

"Just keep quiet," Pinky said to Robin in a firm hushed tone, "Don't say nothing."

"Okay," Robin tried to whisper back.

"Okay you two, let's have a seat," the guard said as he let Pinky go and pointed to some seats for them to take. Pinky didn't take a seat; she just stepped to the side and started pouting and acting up. Robin looked at Pinky and tried to do the same thing, but it was obvious she didn't know how to "act up!"

"Were you two here trying to shoplift?" the guard asked them, looking at Robin. Robin turned her eyes away from him and looked at Pinky's sneakers. The officer noticed and asked Pinky "Did you steal those sneakers?"

"No! No, I ain't steal no sneakers!" Pinky answered, trying to sound like she was upset for being accused.

"What about you young lady, were you trying to steal from my store?"

At first Robin tried not to answer like Pinky had told her.

"Hey! Do you hear me talking to you?! Do you want me to call the police and have them take you to jail?! I'm talking to you!" he said, raising his voice and really putting the fear of God in Robin.

"NO SIR! We didn't steal from your store! My sister got new clothes yesterday and I wanted some. She brought me here to let me try them on 'cause tomorrow we gonna see my mom at the hospital," she mumbled.

"What? Say that again! What are you doing tomorrow?"

"Tomorrow, we gonna see our mother. She is in the hospital and I want to look nice, like my sister,"

"Well how was she gonna make you look nice?"

"She said I could make believe, and the next time she gets paid she gonna buy me something. Just like she bought for her," Robin said. Pinky was listening and too surprised to say anything. She just listened, thinking to herself, 'this girl sure can lie!'

"Is this true?" the security guard asked, turning to Pinky.

"Yes, it's true," Pinky said, with her head hanging down, looking sorry and pitiful.

"What kind of work do you do?"

"She runs errands and cleans for our neighbor Mrs. James," Robin rushed to say.

"Oh really?" said the guard, "And when exactly did you buy these clothes?"

"Yesterday, I bought them yesterday before I got my hair done," Pinky said and she showed him her hair with a great big smile.

"Oh, I see," he said again, "Your hair looks very nice," he added.

"Thank you," Pinky said, as she dug in her pocket and pulled out the balled up receipt. "I don't steal, and I'm sorry", she started to cry. Robin turned and hugged her and she started to cry.

"Alright now, there will be none of that! Hush your crying now, both of you!" he said, passing Pinky back the receipt. "Okay now. No harm has been done, but you cannot come into my store and try on stuff without an adult, even if you do have money," he said, as he turned and looked at Pinky. "I'm gonna have to call someone to come and get you, otherwise I'm gonna have to turn you over to the police."

"But why, we didn't do nothing," Pinky started to pout and cry. "Our grandmother doesn't do anything for us. That's why I brought her here and let her play. We said we were sorry! Our grandmother won't come for us. She doesn't like us!"

"And she's gonna whoop us if you say we were stealing; which we didn't," Robin pleaded as she joined Pinky in starting to cry again.

"Okay, alright, what did I say about that crying? You two are big girls. If you didn't do anything wrong, you don't have anything to cry about. Hush now," he said, as he looked at them questioningly.

"I still need to call her. What's her number?" the security guard said.

"She don't have a phone. can I give you our neighbor's phone number and she can go get her?" Robin asked.

"Sure, what is the number?"

"Murray- 6473, Mrs. James."

"Oh, the lady you work for? What are your names by the way?"

"My name is Robin and hers is Pinky," Pinky said quickly, as he dialed Mrs. James number.

"Hello, is this Mrs. James? My name is Mr. Edwards. I'm calling from Two Guys Department Store and I have two young ladies here who say that their grandmother is your neighbor. Their names are Robin and Pinky. Do you know these young ladies?"

"Yes Sir, I know them. Their grandmother lives upstairs. Would you like for me to send for her? Chances are she won't come to the phone though, you know how that is," Mrs. James offered.

The security guard looked surprised and stared at the girls. "Oh, I see," he said. "Well tell me this, do one of them work for you sometimes, to earn a little money?"

"Yes! That would be Robin; that dear heart. She tries so hard to help out with her sisters. Their mom is in the hospital, you know. Poor thing, no one knows when she'll be home. The girls are going to see her tomorrow as a matter of fact. Would you like for me to send for their grandmother?"

"No, no ma'am, not this time. You've been a big help. Thank you."

"You are welcome. Have a good evening!"

"You too!" Then he hung up the phone and stared at the two girls, so small, so innocent looking and his heart took pity on them. "Let me see that receipt again," he said holding his hand out to Pinky. She gave it to him right away. "So which of these two things did you like trying on the most?" he said to Robin, thinking he was talking to Pinky.

"I like the sneakers," Robin said shyly.

"They look like the ones Robin has on?"

"Yes, just like them," Robin said, again mumbling.

"Well, I tell you what I'm going to do, and I don't usually do this, but . . . I'm going to give you the money Robin, so you can buy the sneakers for your sister. But I want you two to promise 'you will never come here to shop without an adult again'. Is that a promise?"

"Yes!" said Robin

"Yes!" said Pinky who was acting like Robin as the security guard pulled a five dollar bill from his pocket and placed it in her hand!

"This is because I understand that your sister here tries very hard to help out with you while your mother is in the hospital and I remember when I had to step up as the young man of the house and help my mother with my brothers and sisters. It's not easy," he said as he looked at Robin. "Listen to your sister and be good. Alright?"

"Alright Sir!" Robin said as Pinky was pulling her to leave. "You have a very nice store!" Robin added. The security guard just smiled.

"We will!" Pinky said as she was rushing to leave.

As they were leaving Pinky was pulling Robin towards the automatic doors to leave and Robin stopped her.

"What?" Pinky asked.

"What about the sneakers?"

"You still want them? I just want to leave."

"Yes! I want them! And now we don't have to steal them!" Robin said, feeling proud.

"Alright then! Let's go get them! And with all of the lying we just did, and that jacket, we are too stealing. 'Once a thief, always a liar', like Dorothy always says."

"Oh!" Robin said as they went and bought her the pair of sneakers!

Chapter 11

Finally, it was the big day of the trip to see Dorothy. Unbeknownst to the children, Mrs. McMillan had invited Marybelle to come along. She had almost insisted on it to help chaperone the children. Marybelle declined, sending Aunt Valerie to go in her place. Aunt Valerie had just turned 18 a couple of weeks earlier, so she was only too happy to use her "adulthood" to help out with her sister's family. Besides, the trip to the state hospital was two hours away, and would do everyone some good.

The children could have worn Mrs. McMillan out if she didn't have Aunt Valerie and the "each one take responsibility for the next" procedure in place. Whenever the children got too antsy someone would reign them in. Robin was good at coming up with songs and games and Pinky was good at making them listen. Zachary was helping with reading the signs and passing out snacks and lunch. Marybelle had packed everyone bologna sandwiches, apples, and a thermos of half sweetened lemonade. Everyone truly had a good time on the way to the hospital. Once there, the children hardly noticed how big the buildings were nor had they paid attention to the lengthy process the caseworker and Valerie had to go through to get them inside. They were all just excited and anxious to see their mother; but they had no concept of time. After everyone cleared security a hospital attendee led them through two long corridors to another building with tall ceilings and big metal doors. Finally they came to a room labeled "Family Lounge". Inside the lounge, which was a very large rectangular room, there were six 3 metal seat sofas and six metal seat arm chairs all painted a dark forest green and set up like three seating areas. There were three large family style dinner tables suitable for families to crowd around. As this was Dorothy's first visit with all of her six children after two years, there were two nurses behind a partitioned wall sitting at another one of the family style tables, and two more hospital attendees on hand to assist with the visit. Everyone was on standby. As the caseworker had arranged for the visit ahead of time, only Dorothy and her children were in the space for the visit.

When the children came into the room their mother was already there. She was sitting at one of the tables with her hands folded on it. At first all of the children just stared at their mother. There was no way of knowing if any of the children remembered how their mom had looked before she was taken away. But her looks had changed. First off, Dorothy had gained over thirty pounds in her time away. Her hair had been set on sponge rollers in its natural state; not hot combed like she used to wear it. She had on a khaki colored dress and a pair of white boat shoes with ankle socks. She looked beautiful to the children and they looked beautiful to her. Mrs. McMillan, watching quietly, decided to sit and observe the family from a spot on one of the sofas.

"Hi Y'all," Dorothy said quietly excited; breaking the silence!

"Hi Dorothy," Zachary and Pinky said just as excitedly!

"Hi Dorothy," chimed in Rosalyn, with her forever cheerful self!

Ging- Ging waved hello and Dunk just stood swirling from side to side.

Dorothy waved back at Ging-ging and then Dunk as she turned to Robin.

"I don't get a hello? How are you doing?"

"Yes, of course," Robin said as she walked with her arms outstretched to give her mother a hug. Dorothy didn't stand but she let Robin hug her and then started to cry as she hugged her back. All of a sudden the children flocked to their mother to get in on the hugs; even Dunk, who Dorothy picked up and sat on the table in front of her.

"Hi Dunk, how are you?" Dorothy asked, tugging gently at Dunk's cheek.

"I three," she said, holding up her fingers to show.

"Yes, I know," Dorothy said, kissing her little fingers, "you three!"

"You Momma," Dunk said as she reached out and touched Dorothy on her breast.

"Yes, I'm Momma!" Dorothy said, taking Dunk's hand into hers.

"You Momma!" Dunk said again with a big sigh.

"Yes, I'm Momma!" Dorothy replied looking at Robin questioningly.

"She don't like calling Marybelle 'Momma'," Robin told Dorothy.

"Oh, I see," said Dorothy and she pulled Dunk to her, kissing her gently all about her face. Dunk just giggled and soaked up the overdue show of a mother's affection.

After a few minutes Dorothy turned her attention to her little sister, all grown up!

"So Valerie, you eighteen now. Happy belated Birthday," she said. "I would have sent a card, but you know . . ."

"Oh, yes; eighteen! Shoot... I don't need a card." She said as she waved her hand at the thought. "Thank you! I'll soon be leaving home," Aunt Valerie said.

"Leaving home, why? Are you getting married?" Dorothy teased.

"Married? No, oh gee; no! I just meant I am old enough to leave," Valerie said, waving off the conversation.

"Oh, but are you looking to get married to; what's his name? Herman?" Dorothy asked.

"Oh No! Dorothy! Please stop! He is old news anyway," Valerie said as she laughed out loud.

Dorothy smiled a warm smile of adoration and appreciation for her sister. Then she turned her attention back to the children.

"So Zachary, look how tall and handsome you are! What are you up to?"

"Nothing much," Zachary said, feeling bashful about receiving the compliment. "I stay at Aunt Marsha's hanging out with the boys a lot. Their uncle likes to take us fishing. He said he might take me hunting with them come the fall."

"Hunting? Like with a rifle? You best be careful hanging out around rifles, you hear?"

"Yes Ma'am, I will," he said.

"Come here Rosalyn," she said as she noticed Rosalyn slipping off to the side. "How are you doing? Why are you trying to hide?"

"I'm not hiding. I'm looking to see if you really crazy. You not being crazy to me."

Zachary, Pinky, and Robin all froze at Rosalyn's remarks; horrified for their mom. Mrs. McMillan hearing the child sat up straight, poised to take the children and run if necessary, it seemed. As Mrs. Mc Millan sat up, the attendees in the room also gave pause.

But to everyone's surprise and delight Dorothy just retorted with, "Well what does crazy look like to you?"

"It looks like this," Rosalyn said as she began to swing her head from side to side and make stupid sounds with her lips! Dorothy started laughing as she reached out and pulled Rosalyn close. "Well; see then, I'm not crazy, but you are," and she tickled Rosalyn until tears came into her eyes from laughing and she pleaded for her mother to stop.

Rosalyn had broken the ice and chased the elephant out of the room!

Dorothy had the children all take seats at the table and then said to them "Listen; I know that you all are probably wondering what is wrong with me. I am too. The doctors say I have something called Schiz-o-phren-ia," she said phonetically! "Excuse me," Zachary said, "What is Schizo..."?

"Schizophrenia" Dorothy finished for him. "It is something that happens in my mind that makes me hear and see things that are not seen and heard by anyone else. But if I take my medicine I won't hear or see things again! But I need to be with you all. Y'all the best medicine for me and I miss y'all so much she said. Every day I have to take my medicine. But you know what I told those doctors and nurses?" Dorothy asked. "I told them I need to be with my children. I told them you all are the best medicine for me and they have to let me go home to be with y'all!" The children squealed with delight at what their mother had told the doctors and nurses. Then she said to them "What you say, can I come home and y'all be my medicine?" The children filled the room with an explosion of yeses and yays as the children showed how happy they would be if their mother could come home. The happiness and joy of the family was contagious as even the nurses and attendees smiled to hear the different bits and pieces of conversations and expressions of love and happiness.

The rest of the afternoon continued to go pretty much like that until the nurse came and told Dorothy her time was almost up. She asked Mrs. McMillan if she could have a moment alone with Pinky and Robin. Mrs. McMillan said "Of course!"

"Pinky! Robin! I want to tell you two something. Of all of y'all I am most worried about you two. I understand that I took you two with me and you must have seen some scary things, yes?"

"Not so scary," said Pinky.

"Yeah, not so scary," said Robin following her big sister's lead.

"Well it was pretty scary for me, let me tell you. I called it 'my monster' and I'm sorry for having let you two see it. Do you two want to talk about that day?" Dorothy waited, looking at the girls as if to see a sign or something. At first it seemed as if they had nothing to say, but then Robin asked "Why do you call it your 'monster'?"

"Yes, why do you call it 'a monster'?" Pinky also asked, wanting to know.

"I call it a monster because it was very scary and it came out whenever it wanted to. When I first got here it wouldn't go away and I was just scared all the time. But now I take my medicine and the monster has been gone for a while now! It made me so mad and sad that I had you two with me and couldn't take care of you two. I'm sorry, I'm so, so sorry that you had to see all of that."

"You were not a monster to us, right Pinky?" Robin said. "I was scared but Pinky knew what to do. She crossed us across the street and got us home!"

"Yeah you weren't a monster to me! Monsters? I've seen monsters on tv and they scare me to death. You didn't scare us, not until they had to tie you up and take you away," Pinky said as her voice started to trail off.

"Yeah . . ." Dorothy said as she pulled the two girls close to her and hugged them tightly. They all cried silently; each, seemingly, to themselves.

As Dorothy pulled back and looked them in the face she said, "Y'all keep taking care of each other and look out for your little sisters, okay? I hear that you two are doing a great job helping! Thank you, thank you for being my "Big Girls!" Alright?"

"Yes!" the girls said proudly in unison.

"See! I told you. If this is crazy; it's alright with me!" Pinky said to Robin. To her mother, she said, "I told Robin we are all a little crazy just like you and I don't mind. I will fight anybody that makes me mad or tries to hurt anybody in our family. So I'm already crazy and I don't care!"

"Well I want you to care, Pinky," Dorothy said smiling, as she drew Pinky closer to her. "You are a young lady and you are going to have to remember to always act like one. Why, just look how pretty you look today! Who did your hair?" Dorothy asked, really noticing Pinky in that moment. So much so that she made her daughter blush with pride.

"Gloria did it. Thank you!"

"Well you certainly are welcome and you are not crazy. Okay?"

"Okay!" Pinky agreed with a head nod. But secretly she knew that she had no problem being 'just like her mother' whatever that would mean!

"I also see that you all are remembering to use your manners. That's good. Y'all make me so proud!"

"'Always remember your manners: They will carry you far in life,' that's what you said." Robin told her mother.

"Yes! That's what I said. And it's the truth!" Dorothy said, delighted as she pulled the two young girls to her and gave them both a squeeze and hug. They felt so good. They loved their mother and she loved them. That day, they were allowed to remember and to simply be their mother's "little girls".

"When are you coming home?" Pinky asked.

"I don't know yet. But I told the doctor 'you all are the medicine that I need', so hopefully very soon. They say that I still have to learn more about living with Schizophrenia. I'm learning as quickly as I can and as well as I can so I can hurry home to you all. I also have to work on my getting mad. Getting angry and upset may make the "monster" come back." Dorothy said; giving Pinky a special look. We have to learn how to handle our anger. It's not a good thing to have it taking control and making us fight."

Pinky looked down a little embarrassed.

Robin asked, "For real?" picturing a big old ugly monster's face on her mother. "Well we will just have to beat him up," Robin said showing her mother her fists. "Pinky can you show us how to fight the monster and beat him up!"

Pinky looked afraid and said "I'm scared of monsters. I don't think I can beat them; but we love you!"

Dorothy burst out with a very hearty laugh at Pinky's expressions and words as she stood up, putting her hands around her "Big Girls'" shoulders and started walking them over to the others who had been cleaned up and prepared to go. Robin looked up at her mother and as she listened to her mother's laughter she smiled and thought she had never seen or heard that before. She had no recollection of her mother ever laughing. She didn't know why or understand it, but this was proof to her that her mother's monster was definitely gone. What a wonderful sound to her and she wanted to make sure she remembered that sound of laugher forever!

Another round of hugs and goodbyes and the visit came to an end. The ride home started out with so much silence; everyone remembering the visit as if it had been one on one with each one of them separately. Dorothy looked well. Somehow, it had seemed like just yesterday they had last seen her. Miss McMillan broke the silence by asking "How do you all feel right now? Is everyone okay?"

"Yes!" the children all said in unison.

"We are okay," Robin said in a low mono-tone, reassuring voice.

Chapter 12

For the next few days the children continued to enjoy the spirit of childhood in which their mother's visit had enveloped them. Pinky visited her sisters a lot more; abandoning her adventures with Jenny and Barbara. Robin was so happy and content to have her sister around, and even Marybelle was more pleasant toward her as Pinky stayed in the place of a little girl.

After the visit with their mother, it was as if time sped forward so there was talk of their mother coming home. It was as if, for Robin, that the idea that her mother was coming home signaled that she must begin to stray away from the adventures with her sister and get back to being the well behaved, "good little girl," her mother expected her to be. It was going to be hard to give up her adventures with Pinky! They had, very quickly, become the highlight of her days, weeks, and months at her grandmother's house.

It was a nice Saturday morning as evidenced by the summer breeze blowing at the beautiful plastic curtains hanging from the open screened in windows. Add the sound of the music from the radio playing from the kitchen and you have a calling to an adventurous spirit in the little girl named Robin... She had awakened early but yet late as she had found Pinky preparing to leave the house.

"Where are you going?" she asked Pinky.

"I don't know," Pinky said, "I think' I'll just go walking."

"May I go with you?" Robin asked.

"I guess so, if you want," Pinky said.

"Can we eat some cereal first?" Robin asked.

"I already ate," said Pinky, "I'll go find Jenny and Barbara and I'll come back for you; alright?"

"Alright!" Robin said as she prepared a bowl of corn flakes for herself. Robin ate the bowl of cereal rather quickly and decided that she would leave and catch up to Pinky. Sure enough, just as Robin reached the corner of Ege at Jackson Avenue, she walked right into the three girls. She greeted Jenny and Barbara and again asked Pinky, "Where are we going?"

"We are going to walk on the railroad tracks!" Pinky said excitedly.

"Yes! This is going to be fun!" said Jenny, as they turned back up Ege Avenue towards Bergen Avenue.

Robin thought to herself, "this gotta be cool, but how are we going to get way down there where the tracks are?" She kept her thoughts to herself, because she knew by now that her sister and her friends usually had everything figured out.

At Bergen the girls climbed a little concrete wall that acted as a barrier. It was made of concrete encrusted with little stones and pebbles that Robin did not like touching. The roughened, textured wall was challenging to all the girls so Pinky told Robin to "Be careful and follow me" as she walked down a little hill on the side that led to a walkway under an overpass. It was a bridge, with a grated floor, that actually hung above the tracks. Workmen used this bridge when there was work to be done on the train from above or on the tracks. The girls were having a great time! Robin thought to herself how exciting it all was! She still had her fears and concerns but she had learned to trust Pinky and Jenny so much that she kept her fears in check and her concerns to herself; like, "How will we get down to the tracks?" No sooner thought than Jenny was heading down another path on the opposite side of the track. A hill similar to the one they came down to get to the bridge. They still had to hold on to bushes and feel their way along the wall when it lent itself, but soon the girls were right down on the very ground that the tracks ran across. Robin was totally amazed that they had gotten down there. She looked up and could hardly recognize anything about the street above even though she had looked down from that perch many times. For Pinky, Jenny, and Barbara it was nothing special anymore; they had taken this path plenty of times.

Robin looked one way and the other; as far as she could see in either direction, she saw railroad tracks. She wondered how far these tracks went. Where did people get off and on? That's what she did from time to time, just wondered about things. No sooner had she begun to wonder she heard her sister calling out to her; "Come on, Robin! Keep up!" After a while they took a shortcut, crossed over to the other side of the tracks, and were going up another short hill to come out of the "cuts."

"Wow! That was so much fun!" Robin said. The other girls just chuckled. Robin was so easy to impress.

"Yeah, it was all right!" Pinky said as she grabbed her little sister around the neck like she normally did. She loved impressing her little sister. She loved that there were so many things her sister did not know and was so easy to amaze! She held her a little closer, as if she could actually love her any more than she did right now . . .

After walking a block or two Jenny called back to Pinky "You all want to go get a couple of dollars?" she asked as she nodded her head towards a set of buildings. Barbara shrugged an alright with her. Pinky looked at Robin and back at Jenny and Barbara questioningly. Then she shrugged her shoulders and said "Alright . . ." too.

"Alright then, let's go," Jenny said.

They cut through the back of one block and ended up coming out on the front of another. There were a number of car garages where some mechanics were working, and some of them were fooling around. As the girls were walking toward the garages an old man called out "Hey!" to the girls. Pinky and Jenny waved at him as they steered their walk to join up with the man. Soon two other men joined the old man and they all stepped into the garage, each one then stepping off into their own spaces. The old man sat down on an old worn out chair and leaned on a table as Jenny and Pinky stepped ahead of Barbara and Robin to speak with the man. The old man looked around the garage and nodded at the other two men who nodded back. He held up two of his fingers and each man pulled out two dollars; holding them up for the girls to see. The girls smiled and nodded at the men. One man pointed to Barbara and the other pointed to Jenny. Jenny and Barbara went over to the men who beckoned them while the old man whispered to Pinky and pointed to Robin. He pulled out more singles. Pinky put up her hand and waved Robin to come to her. When Robin walked over to Pinky she glanced over and saw that Jenny and Barbara were being groped by the men who had pointed to them. She was shocked and surprised to see this but still she came close to Pinky who had not yet been touched. "What?" Robin said to Pinky as she quietly hoped that Pinky was not about to let the dirty looking old man with his oil stained, blackened hands touch her body.

But of course that's what Pinky was calling Robin over for as she said to her, "Come here. He wants to touch us together and he is going to give us five dollars to share!" As Pinky was explaining what was about to take place, the old man reached forward, took Robin by the wrist and pulled her close to him. Pinky stepped in between the man's leg, her back to Robin and the man. The old man took his free hand and started groping Pinky. Robin began to feel sick as she looked at the man's filthy, blackened hands touching her sister. All the while he never let go of Robin's arm, and after a minute he twisted Robin into the tight space left between his legs where she became trapped back to back with her sister. The dirty old man groped both of them... Robin stood there in total shock! She thought she would pee in her pants if she did not get away. Pinky was not phased at all, nor was she responsive. After a second or two he gave her the singles from the table and gently pushed her away. Pinky stepped a few feet from him and turned to watch as he continued to molest Robin. As she noticed the look of horror on Robin's face she realized that Robin wasn't prepared for this! She walked over to the man and attempted to pull Robin away from him. He laughed as he grabbed Robin's arm for just a second, making Pinky have to pull at her harder. He let Robin go and told Pinky, "Don't bring her around here again, next time I won't be so easy on her!"

Robin, now free, took off running down the block with Pinky running and calling after her. "Robin, Robin wait up! Come here. Wait up!" But Robin could not hear her sister. She had been mortified and defiled. She just wanted to go somewhere and hide. She was confused and full of shame.

Robin ran from the corner of Bergen and Virginia Avenues and had almost made it to the corner of Ege and Jackson when Pinky finally caught up to her. Jenny and Barbara were right behind them.

"What's wrong?" Pinky asked, "Why did you leave us like that?"

"'Cause she is a brat," Jenny said looking from Robin to Pinky.

"That's why I keep telling you, she can't do everything we do! But you don't listen. She got us running down the street, making people look at us like we done robbed somebody.

She makes me sick!" Jenny said, thoroughly upset over the matter.

"Yeah? Well sometimes you make me sick!" Pinky said to Jenny. "How you gonna get mad at her because she didn't like that. I remember when we first started doing it. I didn't like it either. I still don't like it, do you? We just do it now for a couple of dollars here and there. Maybe next time . . ."

"There ain't gonna be no next time! I don't care what you say. She ain't coming with us. Or you can hang with her by yourself. What do you say Barbara ?" Jenny asked.

"Wait a minute can I say something?" Robin interjected.

"What?!" Jenny retorted, frightening Robin.

"I'm sorry! I was scared and I didn't like that. I'm sorry for running and I'm sorry for making you all mad. Don't be mad at Pinky, and Pinky please don't be mad at Jenny. You two are so cool and you are best friends. Jenny is right Pinky, I can't go everywhere you go and I can't do everything you do. I don't even want to . . ." Robin said, hanging her head down low, feeling ashamed.

"See?!" Jenny said looking at Pinky, "she knows what I'm talking about! Okay then Robin, you are okay with me; how about you Barbara?"

Barbara just hunched her shoulders and made a face signifying that she was alright with whatever Jenny was alright with. Between them, as cousins, it was always like that.

"Just one thing:" Jenny started, "You gonna tell anybody what we did? You feeling 'ashamed' and all . . . You gonna tell your grandmother? 'Cause you can't tell anybody, not even your momma -your real momma -your mother! You gotta swear not to tell or God may strike you dead!"

Robin looked at Pinky, who was looking somewhat confused about everything, but seemed to also want to know. Then she looked back between Barbara and Jenny. She knew she wasn't going to tell her grandmother or anyone else, they didn't matter so much; but to "swear" not to tell her mother. How could she? What if her mother asked? These were Robin's thoughts as she heard Jenny asking again, "Well? Are you? Are you going to tell anybody?"

"No. No I won't tell anybody," Robin said in a quiet voice; a voice full of fear and doubt.

"You swear?" Jenny asked.

Robin hesitated to answer, so Jenny went to ask again with some forcefulness. Pinky stepped between them and took Robin by the shoulders. "You swear?" Pinky asked, "You gotta swear or I won't . . . 'we' won't believe you!"

"I swear!" Robin said adamantly, now holding her head up and looking into her sister's face and eyes searching for some assurance of her own; assurance that they were still going to be "best big sister, little sister ever"; like they were still going to take adventures, and most importantly, that Pinky still loved her . . .

Try as she might; having stared as hard as she could, there was no assurance, there was nothing familiar. Robin could tell that something had changed in Pinky toward her, but she could not figure out what, why, or how.

Chapter 13

Pinky did not go back to Marybelle's house after that day. She went back to staying at different people's houses. Robin went back to looking after her little sisters and running errands. After a week or so Robin was happy when Marybelle sent her to go get Zachary and Pinky again. Mrs. McMillan was coming over. When she and Zachary finally caught up with Pinky, Robin was really happy to see her! "Hi Pinky! Guess what? I got some finger nail polish! You want me to polish your nails? I polished ours (meaning their little sisters) already," she said holding her hands out for Pinky to see. "No!" Pinky said as she pushed Robin hands down and turned her attention to Zachary.

"What do you think Mrs. McMillan wants this time? You think she is coming to tell us Dorothy is coming home?" Pinky asked him.

"Probably," Zachary said, oblivious to the exchange between his two sisters.

But Robin wasn't oblivious, she was surprised to see that her sister was still acting different towards her. Robin did not expect it and she wasn't sure why Pinky was doing it!. She dug in her pocket and pulled out 3 pieces of Bazooka bubble gum and tried to pass them out.

"You want one?" she offered to Zachary and Pinky.

"Sure," Zachary said. "Thank you!"

"No!" Pinky said as she again pushed her hand away.

Robin now knew for sure that her sister was still upset with her! Robin felt sick, heart broken! She fell behind Zachary and Pinky and finished the walk back to their grandmother's house saddened and in silence. Pinky had assumed right! Mrs. McMillan had come to tell the children that their mother would be coming home in two weeks!

The children made such a ruckus jumping up and down and dancing with each other that, for a split second, it seemed as if Pinky was no longer behaving differently toward Robin. She grabbed her, but then just as quickly, pushed her away and grabbed Rosalyn instead, and twirled her around. Robin was devastated.

Weeks had passed and, having spent no time with Pinky and going on no adventures to entertain herself, Robin was becoming quite moody and easily agitated. She was mean to everyone and just wanted to hurt somebody; but she didn't know why. She had been traumatized by the ordeal with "the dirty old man" and her hero was not available to talk about it with. On one of these days Nita asked Robin to go to the store.

"You want me to go to the store? You paying?" Robin asked; "'Cause if you not you can just get out of my face!" Robin said, showing that she was not in any mood to be messed with.

"Yes; I got a dime for you," Nita said quietly.

Robin held her hand out for the dime and Nita gave it to her without hesitation.

"Okay; what you want?" Robin asked.

Nita gave Robin $0.30 cents for a milk bar, five Maryjane's, a bag of chips and some two-for-a-penny butter cookies.

"Hurry back, please?" Nita asked nicely.

"Sure," Robin said despondently. Her mind was nowhere and everywhere. She barely heard Nita; and furthermore, she also really didn't care.

As she got to the bottom landing of the steps, Mrs. James called to her through her open door. "Hi Robin! Can you go to the store? I need some bread and cheese. I'm going to make grilled cheese for these children."

"Sure," Robin said again with just a tiny bit more oomph then she had for her aunt.

"Hey Sweetie! What's wrong?" asked Mrs. James.

"Nothing," Robin said, her head hanging down, looking pitiful.

"Come here," Mrs. James said as she walked to the door and ushered Robin into a sun-filled room, closing the door behind them.

"You sit down now and tell an old woman what is going on," Mrs. James said in such a caring, motherly, concerned voice it just broke Robin down to her core. Robin started crying in soft whimpers, mad that she was crying without even knowing why!

"There, there now," Mrs. James said, "What is going on?" she asked as she lifted Robin's little face which caught the sun.

She pulled a handkerchief from her duster and started wiping Robin's eyes and cheeks ever so gently.

"I don't know," Robin said as she hunched her little shoulders. "I don't know!"

"Oh my! Well sometimes we feel upset and don't know why," said Mrs. James reassuringly. "That certainly is possible," she said as she wiped Robin's face again, to which Robin pulled away in embarrassment.

"It's okay," Mrs. James said assuringly. "It's okay to let someone help you every now and then. You can't always do for others and not have anyone do for you, it will make you mad and you will go bonkers! You take it from me, you hear?"

"Yes Ma'am," Robin said, forcing a smile as a way of saying thank you; to which she added "Thank you, Mrs. James, I feel better. What would you like from the store?"

"You sure? Because it can wait, believe me, it can wait!"

"No, I'm sure. I'm okay, besides I was already on my way to the store for Nita. I gotta hurry."

"Oh, okay," said Mrs. James; "I just want a quarter pound of cheese and a loaf of bread and you get yourself something, okay?" and she gave Robin a dollar bill.

Robin, feeling better, ran to the store on Bergen and Kearney to get Nita's stuff. She was able to get the cheese from there but they did not have any bread so Robin decided to go down Kearny Avenue to get the bread from Farmingdale's. By the time she got to the store she felt the brown bag was getting wet. When she looked inside she saw that Nita's ice cream bar was melting! She pulled the ice cream on a stick from the bag in its opened wrapper. At first Robin seemed to be somewhat mesmerized at how it was turning all brown and white and liquidity as the melting ice cream was mingling with the melting chocolate coating. Then she started licking the sweet cream and chocolate from her hand! Finally, she told herself that she needed to go on and eat the thing or it was just going to keep on melting all over her. So she did! Then she stuck the stick back into the slip on wrapper and put the wrapper back into the bag so she could show Nita that it had indeed melted. She bought the bread and walked up Ege Avenue back to the house.

She didn't buy anything for herself with the dime that Nita had given her, nor did she buy anything from the dollar that Mrs. James had given her. Mrs. James gave her a quarter from the change. She put the $0.35 cents in her shoe and took Nita her stuff.

"Hey! Where's my milk bar? What is this?" Nita asked as she examined the empty wrapper with the stick in it.

"It melted," Robin said ever so calmly.

"Melted?"

"Yeah. See in the bag?" Robin said, pointing at the bag.

"I see it! It looks like it melted some, but where is the rest of it?" Nita said, still examining the wrapper like she could not believe her eyes. "Did you eat my ice cream?" she said as she grabbed Robin and shoved her up against the wall.

"NO!" Robin yelled at her as she pushed her backwards, "It melted like I said!"

"Well you need to give me back my dime. I paid for it. You should have brought it back here before it melted. I'm gonna tell Momma!" Nita threatened through squinted eyes.

"Tell, I don't care! I don't have no dime and I didn't eat your ice cream. Next time go to the store for yourself!" Robin said; "Besides, remember when I went to the store and you didn't pay me. You can keep *that* dime." With that Robin turned around and went back out the door, leaving Nita to figure out what really happened to her milk bar and whether or not Robin cared in the least.

Chapter 14

Finally, just days before school was to start back Dorothy was home with her children. They all, including Zachary and Pinky, crowded into her mother's house for the first four nights. On the fifth night Zachary asked if he could spend the night at Aunt Marsha's and Pinky just didn't come to the house. Dorothy learned that this was the way Pinky did things, "she comes and goes as she pleases", Marybelle had explained. Dorothy figured she was going to have to hurry and find a place of their own, even though the doctors had advised her to take things slowly.

One morning Dorothy wandered into the kitchen while Marybelle was there having a cup of coffee. "Good morning," Dorothy said to her mother.

"Good morning, would you like a cup of coffee?" Marybelle asked.

"Yes, I think I would," Dorothy said as she proceeded to take a cup, saucer, and spoon from the dish rack. As she sat down to the table with the cup of dark hot liquid, Marybelle slid the tray holding the sugar bowl and creamer towards Dorothy.

"Thank you, and thank you for keeping my children while I was away. I hope they weren't too much of a problem or distraction from you living your life," Dorothy said.

"You are welcome. No, they were alright. You did a fine

job on them with their manners so who could complain; and what good would it do! I'm sorry Pinky and Zachary didn't want to stay, but you can understand. It's so crammed in here. I couldn't blame them," Marybelle said.

Dorothy glanced around looking at all of the familiar clutter that had been around for as long as she could remember.

"Well, never you mind. I'm already looking for a place. We should be gone within a few days."

"Oh! I didn't know that, you sure? I thought -I assumed- it would take you a few months at least," Marybelle said.

"Yeah ... no ... everyone keeps telling me to take it slow, but I have to get my children back together under one roof so I can get back to being their mother," Dorothy said. "I need to get Pinky under control; she's trying to run wild!"

"Yes, I know what you mean," Marybelle mumbled as she put her cup to her mouth and took a big sip, trying to hide the expressions on her face. Dorothy caught the jist of what she said and decided that she would ignore that, as she, too, lifted her cup to her mouth and stared at her mother over the rim of her cup.

It was as if Marybelle could tell what types of thoughts Dorothy was having as she offered, "I'm sorry I could not get down there to see you while you were away. The kids and all . . ." her voice trailed off.

"Yeah, I understand," Dorothy said. "Besides I wouldn't have expected you to come that far to have nothing to say so I was good!"

"Well, you don't know, I might have had plenty to say. Did they figure out what happened to make you, you know . . . go crazy," asked Marybelle.

"They helped me to understand a few things, and at the core of most of my issues was a cry, or shall I say 'longing' for love and concern; which I feel I never got. Certainly you never showed it or gave it to me. Can you imagine that

Momma? If you don't show a child that you love them or at the very least, care about what happens to them, it messes them up. Maybe even makes them go crazy," Dorothy said in almost whispered tones as she rested her cup on the saucer.

"I can very well imagine," Marybelle said, amusing herself. "I know that you and I have had a strained relationship most of your life, but it's not like it was all my fault! You were just so difficult, so different. You were always different, and for all we know you could have been crazy all along! It just decided to explode inside of you."

"Really Marybelle, is that what you need to tell yourself to be able to live with yourself? To be okay with the awful ugly things you've done to me all of my life?" Dorothy asked, her voice elevating. "You hated me so much for being born with dark skin that you abandoned me to your mother, and there you would've left me, had she not brought me up here to you when I was three years old! And what did we find when we got here? You married, and with two more children. You were never going to come and get me, or send for me, were you? You were probably hoping your mother would never have raised enough money to get me on that Greyhound. Did you Marybelle, did you wish I had never come? I just want to hear you admit it just once . . ."

Marybelle put her cup down rather deliberately and quietly pushed back her chair so she could stand as she prepared to respond to her daughter 'once and for all'. "Yes! If you must know; if you really want to know; I would have left you with her forever. I didn't plan to have you. You were just a mistake! So I left and I came north. I had things to do . . . I had dreams I wanted to pursue. What do you think? Because I had you I should not have had a life?"

Marybelle paused just long enough for Dorothy to interject, "No!" she said rather adamantly, "No one would have asked you to 'not have a life". But how could you just leave me and not even look back? How is it that I get here and you have two other children and then two more after that? How do you explain leaving me out of your family for so long? I have six children and there is no way that I can imagine leaving any one of them," Dorothy said exasperated; but grateful to finally be engaged in dialogue with her mother about her lifetime of pain.

"My problem with you is you were always asking these questions, always wanting to know. You whined all the time. You broke up my marriage! My husband lost his trust in me. He felt like I had been dishonest not telling him about you. But how could I? When should I have? And you were always whining, always needy. Had the nerve to make my husband always feel the need to defend you . . . to defend you against me! But what did it get us, you and me? Nothing! He left me. He left because my mother brought you up here. You both ruined my life and so: 'No' I don't have love for you!" Marybelle said loudly as her voice peaked. "And I couldn't have taken you with me! I never would have met my husband had I had you under foot. Besides, my mother wanted to keep you; I didn't make her do that! Truth be told, I wanted to give you away. There was a woman who couldn't have children, she tried and tried with her husband but she just couldn't. But my mother wouldn't let me! Kept talking about how 'you were blood, you were my child and we are a family.' So 'she' kept you. I didn't know that she was waiting for me to 'be ready', to 'change my mind' about you. Had she asked me I would have told her; I did tell her! I never wanted a child, not just you. At that time I didn't want any children. She just didn't listen; and she didn't want to believe me. So there! Are you happy now? Are you satisfied?" Marybelle asked, falling back into her chair as if she had finally been relieved of the burden of 'her truth'.

"No! I am not satisfied," Dorothy said, "but I thank you for finally being honest and admitting to what I've always felt and have always known. All things considered, I wish you would have given me away! It would have been better than feeling thrown away, over and over again, every day of my life! Do you know how often I tried to figure out what I had done? What was so wrong with me? You always made a big deal about the color of my skin but I knew that had to be a lie because Nita and Jacob are the same color and you've never treated them in the ways you've treated me. And as for 'Your husband', as you like to say, he was my father! He loved me. He loved me and he was just as much my father as he was to the rest of them. I thank God for him! He was the only father I ever knew and he never made me feel like I was 'a mistake.' The truth of the matter is, my father did not leave you because of me; he left 'two more' children later because he couldn't put up with your snooty, bougie acting self either! You did not respect him any more than you respected me. In fact you were no different with him than you were with me. You didn't show him any more affection than you showed to me. It seems as though you just wanted his name and loved the idea that he was a hard working, good man. Well, how is it Marybelle that you came all the way up north pretending that I did not exist so you could meet a man and marry and the man ended up loving me more than you did? How is that? And while we are speaking of it, may you please; do tell me who my 'other' father is or anything about him? How did you become pregnant anyway?"

Dorothy paused briefly waiting for a response. When none came she said, "Yeah, I thought not. Everything you've ever said has been nothing but lies. I feel like my whole life is just one big lie; all told to me 'by you as made-up for you'. Damn you!"

Dorothy leaned across the table and looked straight into her mother's eyes as if searching for something, some hope maybe. Finding none, her eyes swelled with water as she said to her mother, "I thank you for keeping my children, I do. But from here on out I want nothing to do with you, not a thing. You didn't want me then. I don't want you now. From this day forward I will tell my own story. I will live my own truth. And in my story 'I don't have a mother!' I never had a mother . . . As far as I am concerned 'I was hatched by a buzzard and raised by the Sun'!"

Marybelle, visibly angered by her daughter's words, felt powerless to defend herself or her position, and stood up to get ready to leave. "So be it," she said. "I'm happy to hear it . . . good riddance to bad rubbish! It surely is about time!"

"Yes it is!" Dorothy said standing up and back, "So, like I said, I am already looking for a place and I will be out of your hair soon enough. Until then, and for the sake of everyone here, let us be respectful and mind our manners towards each other. You just keep your distance and I will keep mine!

Robin, after having heard her mother's voice when it peaked and had been respectfully standing to the side of the kitchen doorway watching and listening to the two women; now came out into the opening of the doorway and stared piercingly at her grandmother. She could not believe or fully understand all that she was hearing but she knew that her grandmother was proving that she had no love for her mother! She could never have ever considered that a mother could have a child and not love it.

Dorothy, noticing Robin, called her to come to her. She saw the hurt and anguish in Robin's face and pulled Robin gently to her. Marybelle looked at Robin with disdain, indignant of the child's emotions.

"Robin? Robin, look at me," Dorothy said in a quiet, gentle voice. "It's okay . . . Look at me," and Robin broke her stare at her grandmother after confirming within herself that she would never forgive her for saying such mean things to her mother.

Once Dorothy had Robin's attention her hands slid down Robin's long slender arms to her long fingers and slender hands saying, "Don't you pay any attention to all of this. This is grown folk's stuff and it doesn't matter what she said. We are going to be moving in just a little while and it's all going to be okay. Do you hear me? It's all going to be okay. For the first time in my life, it's all going to be okay!" Dorothy said as she fell to her knees and burst out with a wail that could have shaken the Rock of Gibraltar loose from its foundation. Dorothy laid her head into Robin's little abdomen as she poured years of hurt and pain out through her cries and tears. Robin put her arms around her mother, half afraid that her mother was going to go crazy again and half filled with anger enough to curse her grandmother, but she couldn't, love or no love Robin knew her mother would not have any of that. After a few minutes that seemed like an eternity to Robin, Dorothy began to calm herself down but not before the other girls came running into the kitchen, one by one, at the sound of her wails. Nita came too, standing at the threshold to the kitchen. She stood watching all of her nieces hovering around their mother, wanting her to be okay. Finally, Dorothy stood up and finished wiping her face with her shirt sleeve.

"Okay, okay," she said, "Enough of all of this crying and carrying on. Who wants to go to the park?"

"I do, I do!" said the girls in unison.

"Okay, let's get ready to go!" Dorothy said as she pushed her girls toward the threshold where Nita was standing. "You want to come?", Dorothy asked Nita.

"Yes," Nita said, half looking at her mother, with shame.

Later that evening, after everyone returned from the park, Robin was still upset about what she had heard spoken between her grandmother and her mother. She needed to talk to Pinky! Besides she just missed her. She went to find her. Pinky was around at the park on Virginia Avenue.

She was there with Jenny, Barbara and another girl named Linda. Robin was afraid to try and talk to Pinky so she just hung out against the pole where Pinky was playing on the swings and talking with her friends.

After a while Pinky came over to Robin and asked, "What's up?"

"Nothing," Robin said with her head hanging down.

"Then why are you here?" Pinky asked.

"Marybelle was mean to Dorothy this morning. It made me mad! And you are the only one I wanted to be around to talk to about it."

"Hold up!" Pinky said, sounding just as upset, "What do you mean 'she was mean'?"

"She told Dorothy that she didn't love her!"

"What?!"

"Yeah! And she made Dorothy cry!" Robin said, her head again, hanging down. "That woman!" Pinky said. "She makes me sick! I don't care what anybody says! I hate her! I do! I hate her! And I can! If she can hate her daughter I can hate her! And I do! Yeah! She hates my mother so I hate her!" Pinky said, pacing back and forth, completely enraged at the thought that someone hurt her mother; even if that someone, and especially since that someone was her mother's own mother.

"Okay! Then I hate her too!" Robin said. "She makes me sick too! How dare she make Dorothy cry!"

"How is she? How is Dorothy?" Pinky asked; her eyes squinty and questioning. In her mind she wanted to know if there were any 'signs of the monster'. Robin understood. She knew because that was her greatest concern too.

"She is okay!" Robin said, showing some glimmer of excitement and hope with the answer. "She took us all to the park!" Robin also said excitedly.

"You had fun?" Pinky asked rubbing Robin across the

top of her head; allowing herself to tap into the feeling of excitement Robin was beginning to generate.

"I had fun but I missed you. I wished you were there with us. That's why I came around here. What about you?" Robin ventured to ask. "You missed me?" she said, hanging her head; hoping her sister had! "I don't know why you don't talk to me anymore. I don't know why you're still mad at me but I am sorry! I am sorry for whatever I did and I want my sister back."

"I'm not mad at you Robin!" Pinky said. "I mean, at first I was. I thought I was; anyway. But not anymore . . . It's just that sometimes you're so different from me and my friends. Every time I let you be or play with us, you always make me feel like you think you are better than us! That's what happens. That's how I feel . . . sometimes!"

"'Think I'm better than you"? Pinky I love you! You're my sister. You Batman, I'm Robin . . . we the dynamic duo. I 'feel' like I'm nothing without you! Without you around I just be scared all the time. Scared of even nothing. You make me think I can do anything! When I hang out with you, there ain't nothing you don't do if you want to! Sometimes I just be a little scared *because* you ain't scared of nothing. Sometimes I'm so scared because I be scared for the both of us! But one thing I know for sure... we will always be alright. You never let anything happen to us. You always get us out of trouble and you are always ready to fight for us. Scared or not, I trust you. I know that because of you, everything will be alright! I don't know what 'think I am better than you' means. When I don't want to do something, it's because I think we are not supposed to. I just don't want us to get in trouble. Because we never do I should stop thinking about it. I'd rather get in trouble with you than to not hang with you at all." Robin said, exasperated and out of breath for pouring out her heart to her beloved sister.

"Robin you are my sister and I love you even if sometimes

you are just too sweet! You're such a 'goody two shoes' and my friends don't like when I bring you around. That's why I haven't bothered with you too much. 'I love you'!" said Pinky.

"I love you too Pinky!"

Pinky pulled her sister near, putting her arm around her neck and drawing her close. "Like old times!" Robin was thinking and 'feeling'!

"Do you want to get on the swings?" Pinky asked.

"Yeah!" Robin said, without hesitation...

Made in the USA
Middletown, DE
13 February 2021